WILLIAMS
SONOMA
—— CALIFORNIA ——

PIZZA

DELICIOUS RECIPES FOR ANYTIME

weldon**owen**

CONTENTS

INTRODUCTION

With a little planning and practice, plus a collection of great recipes, making homemade pizza can be deliciously fun and completely achievable. In fact, it's a party the entire family can take part in. All you really need are a pizza oven or a household oven and pizza stone to create a blistered crisp-and-chewy crust topped with your favorite ingredients. Adventurous cooks can branch out and use their grills for smoke-kissed flavor, or adapt the recipes to a wood-fired outdoor pizza oven or an electric countertop pizza oven.

With this book in hand, you can gather family and friends for a pizza party whenever the inspiration or the craving strikes. Here you'll find easy-to-prepare recipes for doughs, sauces, and toppings, as well as techniques for grilled pizza and calzone. An array of different doughs includes something for everyone—from thin-crust New York style pizza dough and chewy whole wheat dough, to focaccia-like sheet pan pizza dough and cornmeal-flecked deep dish dough that's baked in a cast-iron pan. You'll also find a gluten-free dough and a grain-free cauliflower dough—both can be used with any of the sauce and topping combinations in the book.

Sauces and toppings are simple ways to change up the flavor profiles of any pizza—especially when you use the best ingredients available. The tomato-based All-Purpose Pizza Sauce (page 106) and Basil Pesto (page 109) are tried-and-true favorites, and you can easily add pizzazz with Creamy Garlic Sauce (page 114) or even Barbecue Sauce (page 115).

Cherry tomatoes, asparagus, eggplant, fresh figs, and sweet corn evoke the seasons and give your pizza plenty of personality. White pizzas, like Wild Mushroom, Caramelized Onion & Fontina Pizza (page 29) or Potato & Rosemary Pizza (page 22) are elegant enough for a dinner party. Thick, fluffy, family friendly Mushroom, Pepperoni & Black Olive Sheet Pan Pizza (page 64) can be prepared in advance, making it an easy solution for a weeknight meal, while Grilled Pizza with Prosciutto, Mozzarella & Hot Honey (page 63) will be the star of your summer barbecues. The combination of doughs, sauces, and toppings are endless, so use this book as a guide and create your own favorites.

PIZZA PRIMER

Making pizza at home is easy and doesn't need to be time-consuming or labor-intensive. With just a few tools, a little prep work, and some everyday skills, serving homemade slices is doable on any weeknight schedule. Keep these tips and tricks in mind and you'll create a terrific pizza every time.

Mixing & Kneading

You can prepare any of the top-notch pizza doughs in this book using your hands or an electric stand mixer. A food processor can also make quick work of mixing and kneading the dough. Dough mixed by any of these methods shouldn't vary perceptibly, so choose the technique you prefer.

Rising

After mixing and kneading, yeast doughs need to rise at room temperature for at least 1 hour, or until doubled in size and air bubbles form in the dough. You can also let them rise in the refrigerator overnight. Be sure to let the dough come to room temperature until it looks puffy before using.

Shaping

To preserve the texture and airy nature of the dough, especially with the yeasted doughs, it's best to shape them with your hands instead of using a rolling pin. If the dough starts to spring back, give it a rest. With a little practice, you'll be pulling dough like a pizzaiolo in no time.

Baking

The thin-crust pizza doughs in this book bake best at the highest temperature your conventional oven will go, usually 550°F/290°C. Thicker pizzas, like the sheet pan pizza and deep dish pizza are best baked at a slightly lower temperature, around 450°F/230°C, as is the gluten-free pizza. Be sure to preheat your oven and pizza stone for at least 30 minutes prior to baking.

TOP PIZZA TIPS

Start with top-notch ingredients to guarantee the most tasty results. Buy the best-quality cheese, olive oil, and toppings your budget will allow.

Let your dough rest. If the dough continues to bounce back when you are stretching it out, set it aside to rest for about 10 minutes, then try again.

When adding toppings, leave a 1-inch (2.5-cm) border of bare crust, brushed with olive oil, so the toppings won't escape over the edges during baking.

Don't overtop your pizza before baking, which can yield a gummy crust and floppy slices. Approach your toppings with the "less is more" rule. First, brush the edges lightly with olive oil, then lightly coat all but about a 1-inch (2.5-cm) border of the crust with sauce. Next, sprinkle on the cheese and toppings with a light hand. Keep toppings simple, with no more than three main ingredients.

Preheat the oven and pizza stone. Before baking a pizza, make sure the oven has reached its highest possible temperature and the pizza stone has had time to absorb the heat. If the temperature is too low, the pizza will be undercooked. Resist opening the oven before the suggested baking time has been reached.

Transfer with care. Sliding a pizza off of a peel onto a hot pizza stone can be intimidating. To ensure success, make sure the peel is dusted well with semolina flour before you top it with the dough. If it isn't, when you try to slide the pizza onto the stone, the pie will stick and toppings will go flying. Use a large, flat spatula first to loosen the pizza from the peel and then to guide it into the oven and onto the stone.

Cool slightly before cutting. Once the pizza is out of the oven, let it cool for a few minutes before cutting. This will prevent burned mouths and will keep the melted cheese and toppings from sliding off the slices.

VEGGIE PIZZAS

PESTO PIZZA WITH ZUCCHINI, SWEET CORN & PECORINO

This summery pizza evokes the best of the season, with fresh basil pesto, ribbons of zucchini, and sweet corn kernels. The addition of lemon zest brightens all the flavors of the vegetables. Grated pecorino cheese lends a salty-nutty note, but you can also use shredded mozzarella for a cheesier pie.

Semolina flour, for dusting

One 9-oz (250-g) ball NY Style Pizza Dough (page 98)

Extra-virgin olive oil, for brushing and drizzling

⅓ cup (80 ml) Classic Basil Pesto (page 109)

1 small zucchini, thinly shaved lengthwise

Kosher salt and freshly ground pepper

¼ cup (40 g) fresh corn kernels

¼ cup (30 g) grated pecorino cheese

2 teaspoons grated lemon zest

Flaky sea salt, for garnish

Squash blossoms, for garnish (optional)

MAKES ONE 12-INCH (30-CM) PIZZA; SERVES 2–4

Position an oven rack in the middle of the oven and place a pizza stone on the rack. Preheat the oven to 550°F/290°C (or as high as it will go). Once the oven has reached 550°F/290°C, let the stone continue to heat for 15–30 minutes longer, without opening the door.

On a lightly floured surface, stretch the pizza dough into a 12-inch (30-cm) round. If the dough springs back, let it rest for about 10 minutes before continuing. Dust a pizza peel with semolina and transfer the dough round to the pizza peel.

Brush the edge of the dough round with olive oil. Leaving a 1-inch (2.5-cm) border, spread the pesto over the dough. Arrange the zucchini ribbons on top and season with kosher salt and pepper. Sprinkle with the corn kernels and 2 tablespoons of the cheese.

Carefully slide the pizza from the peel onto the hot stone in the oven and bake for about 8 minutes, or until the crust is golden brown. Using the peel, transfer the pizza to a cutting board and sprinkle with the remaining 2 tablespoons cheese, the lemon zest, and flaky sea salt. Drizzle with olive oil and garnish with squash blossoms, if using. Let cool for about 1 minute, then slice and serve right away.

PESTO, CHERRY TOMATO & MOZZARELLA PIZZA

With only three toppings, this pizza strikes a delicious balance of creamy cheese, juicy tomatoes, and aromatic herbs. You can swap out the basil pesto for Olive Tapenade (page 112), and add dollops of ricotta for equally tasty results.

Semolina flour, for dusting

One 9-oz (250-g) ball NY Style Pizza Dough (page 98)

Extra-virgin olive oil, for brushing

⅓ cup (80 ml) Classic Basil Pesto (page 109)

One 6–8 oz (170–225 g) ball fresh mozzarella cheese, sliced and torn into pieces

6 oz (170 g) cherry tomatoes, halved or quartered if large

Kosher salt and freshly ground pepper

Fresh basil leaves

MAKES ONE 12-INCH (30-CM) PIZZA; SERVES 2–4

Position an oven rack in the middle of the oven and place a pizza stone on the rack. Preheat the oven to 550°F/290°C (or as high as it will go). Once the oven has reached 550°F/290°C, let the stone continue to heat for 15–30 minutes longer, without opening the door.

On a lightly floured surface, stretch the pizza dough into a 12-inch (30-cm) round or oval. If the dough springs back, let it rest for about 10 minutes before continuing. Dust a pizza peel with semolina and transfer the dough round to the pizza peel.

Brush the edge of the dough round with olive oil. Leaving a 1-inch (2.5-cm) border, spread the pesto over the dough and top with the cheese. Scatter the tomatoes over the cheese. Season with salt and pepper.

Carefully slide the pizza from the peel onto the hot stone in the oven and bake for about 8 minutes, or until the crust is golden brown. Using the peel, transfer the pizza to a cutting board. Let cool for about 1 minute, then scatter the basil over the top, slice, and serve right away.

GRILLED PIZZA WITH TOMATOES, RED ONION & ARUGULA

Fire up the grill and wow your friends and family with grilled pizza—a terrific way to entertain. This simply topped pie is a good jumping-off point for getting the hang of it. Partially cooking one side of the pizza ensures that the dough cooks through before the toppings are ready.

Extra-virgin olive oil, for brushing and drizzling

Semolina flour, for dusting

Two 9-oz (25-g) balls NY Style Pizza Dough (page 98) or Whole Wheat Pizza Dough (page 96)

2 cups (230 g) shredded fontina or low-moisture mozzarella cheese

2 ripe but slightly firm heirloom tomatoes, thinly sliced

½ small red onion, cut into paper-thin slices

½ cup pitted and halved black olives (70 g), such as Gaeta or Kalamata

1 cup (35 g) baby arugula

¼ cup (15 g) finely shredded fresh basil

Kosher salt

MAKES TWO 10-INCH (25-CM) PIZZAS; SERVES 4–6

Prepare a gas or charcoal grill for direct and indirect grilling over medium heat (350°–450°F/180°–230°C). Brush the grill grate clean.

Brush two 12-inch (30-cm) squares of aluminum foil on one side with olive oil; place on separate baking sheets. On a lightly floured surface, stretch 1 dough ball into a flat disk. Place in the center of 1 of the foil sheets and stretch the dough into a 10-inch (25-cm) round. Brush the top of the dough all over with olive oil. Repeat with the other dough ball.

Invert 1 dough round directly onto the hotter side of the grill. Using tongs, carefully peel the foil off the dough. Grill with the lid closed for 1–3 minutes, or until the dough is nicely browned on the bottom and almost dry on top. About halfway through (when the dough is cooked enough to move easily), use the tongs to rotate the dough 90 degrees to prevent burning.

Using a pizza peel, transfer the grilled dough round to a cutting board, grilled side up. Repeat with the second dough round.

Brush the grilled tops of both pizzas lightly with olive oil. Leaving a 1-inch (2.5-cm) border, top each with half of the cheese and half of the tomato slices. Scatter half of the onion slices and half of the olives over the tomatoes.

Place 1 pizza on the hotter side of the grill. Cover the grill and cook, rotating the pizza about 90 degrees halfway through, for 1–3 minutes, or until the bottom browns and the cheese starts to melt. Slide the pizza to the cooler side of the grill, cover the grill, and cook for 2–3 minutes longer, or until the cheese finishes melting.

Using the pizza peel, transfer the pizza to the cutting board. Repeat with the second pizza. To serve, top each pizza with half of the arugula and basil. Drizzle with olive oil and sprinkle with salt. Slice and serve at once.

FETA, CHERRY TOMATO & OLIVE TAPENADE MINI PIZZAS

Choose an array of multicolored cherry and grape tomatoes to add eye-catching color to these mini pizzas. The pizza gets a good amount of saltiness from both the feta and the rich olive tapenade, but it's well balanced by the fresh tomatoes and basil. Serve these with the Chopped Salad with Tarragon Buttermilk Dressing (page 87) and a bright red wine.

Two 9-oz (250-g) balls NY Style Pizza Dough (page 98)

Semolina flour, for dusting

Extra-virgin olive oil, for brushing and drizzling

½ cup (120 ml) Olive Tapenade (page 112) or Classic Basil Pesto (page 109)

4 oz (115 g) crumbled feta cheese

About 24 cherry tomatoes, preferably a mixture of colors, halved or quartered if large

6–8 fresh basil leaves, julienned

MAKES EIGHT 6-INCH (15-CM) MINI PIZZAS; SERVES 6–8

Position an oven rack in the middle of the oven and place a pizza stone on the rack. Preheat the oven to 550°F/290°C (or as high as it will go). Once the oven has reached 550°F/290°C, let the stone continue to heat for 15–30 minutes longer, without opening the door.

Divide the pizza dough into 8 equal pieces.

On a lightly floured surface, stretch each piece into a 6-inch (15-cm) round. If the dough springs back, let it rest for about 10 minutes before continuing. Dust a pizza peel with semolina and transfer 2 dough rounds to the pizza peel.

Working with 2 dough rounds at a time, brush each dough round with olive oil. Leaving a ½-inch (12-mm) border, spread about 1 tablespoon of tapenade over each dough round. Sprinkle each with a heaping tablespoon of the cheese and some cherry tomatoes.

Carefully slide the mini pizzas from the peel onto the hot stone in the oven and bake for 4–5 minutes, or until the crust is golden brown. Using the peel, transfer the mini pizzas to a cutting board. Drizzle with olive oil. Let cool for about 1 minute, then scatter basil over the top, slice, and serve.

Repeat to cook the remaining mini pizzas. With practice, you can fit 4 of the pizzas at a time on the stone.

MUSHROOM, ROASTED PEPPER & ARTICHOKE PIZZA WITH ARUGULA

This veggie pizza has it all: tangy artichoke hearts, sautéed mushrooms, sweet roasted peppers, and briny olives, all topped with a tangle of peppery arugula. The mix of ingredients is nicely balanced, but swap out any ingredients you aren't a fan of.

1 tablespoon extra-virgin olive oil, plus more for brushing and drizzling

5 oz (140 g) cremini mushrooms, brushed clean and thickly sliced

Kosher salt and freshly ground pepper

Semolina flour, for dusting

One 9-oz (250-g) ball NY Style Pizza Dough (page 98) or Whole Wheat Pizza Dough (page 96)

1/3–1/2 cup (80–120 ml) All-Purpose Pizza Sauce (page 106)

1 cup (115 g) shredded low-moisture mozzarella cheese

2 tablespoons chopped jarred roasted red bell pepper, drained

4 jarred artichoke hearts, drained and thinly sliced

2 tablespoons pitted and sliced black olives, preferably Kalamata

1 cup (35 g) baby arugula

MAKES ONE 12-INCH (30-CM) PIZZA; SERVES 2–4

Position an oven rack in the middle of the oven and place a pizza stone on the rack. Preheat the oven to 550°F/290°C (or as high as it will go). Once the oven has reached 550°F/290°C, let the stone continue to heat for 15–30 minutes longer, without opening the door.

In a frying pan over medium-high heat, warm the olive oil. Add the mushrooms, season with salt and pepper, and cook, stirring occasionally, for about 4 minutes, or until the mushrooms soften. Remove from the heat and set aside.

On a lightly floured surface, stretch the pizza dough into a 12-inch (30-cm) round. If the dough springs back, let it rest for about 10 minutes before continuing. Dust a pizza peel with semolina and transfer the dough round to the pizza peel.

Brush the edge of the dough round with olive oil. Leaving a 1-inch (2.5-cm) border, spread the sauce over the dough and sprinkle with the cheese. Arrange the mushrooms, roasted peppers, artichoke hearts, and olives over the top.

Carefully slide the pizza from the peel onto the hot stone in the oven and bake for about 8 minutes, or until the crust is golden brown. Using the peel, transfer the pizza to a cutting board. Drizzle with olive oil. Let cool for about 1 minute, then scatter the arugula over the top, slice, and serve right away.

CACIO E PEPE PIZZA

Cacio e pepe—a combination of pecorino cheese and freshly ground black pepper—is a classic Roman pasta dish. Here, we've transformed those flavors into a pizza that is simple but first-rate.

One 6-oz (170-g) ball fresh mozzarella cheese, preferably buffalo, thinly sliced

Semolina flour, for dusting

One 9-oz (250-g) ball NY Style Pizza Dough (page 98)

Extra-virgin olive oil, for brushing and drizzling

⅓ cup (80 ml) Creamy Garlic Sauce (page 114)

¼ cup (30 g) grated pecorino cheese

Freshly ground pepper

MAKES ONE 12-INCH (30-CM) PIZZA; SERVES 2–4

Position an oven rack in the middle of the oven and place a pizza stone on the rack. Preheat the oven to 550°F/290°C (or as high as it will go). Once the oven has reached 550°F/290°C, let the stone continue to heat for 15–30 minutes longer, without opening the door.

If using buffalo mozzarella, spread the pieces on paper towels and blot dry slightly. Set aside.

On a lightly floured surface, stretch the pizza dough into a 12-inch (30-cm) round. If the dough springs back, let it rest for about 10 minutes before continuing. Dust a pizza peel with semolina and transfer the dough round to the pizza peel.

Brush the edge of the dough round with olive oil. Leaving a 1-inch (2.5-cm) border, spread the sauce over the dough and top with the mozzarella and then the pecorino. Season generously with pepper.

Carefully slide the pizza from the peel onto the hot stone in the oven and bake for about 8 minutes, or until the crust is golden brown. Using the peel, transfer the pizza to a cutting board. Drizzle with olive oil. Let cool for about 1 minute, then slice and serve right away.

POTATO & ROSEMARY PIZZA

If you've never had potatoes on pizza, you're in for a treat. The high
temperature of the oven renders the thinly sliced potato golden and crispy.
A layer of sweet caramelized leeks makes a great addition to the pizza.

2 cups (475 ml) water

1 tablespoon kosher salt, plus
more as needed

1 Yukon gold or red potato, very
thinly sliced

1 tablespoon extra-virgin olive oil,
plus more for brushing

Freshly ground pepper

⅓ cup (80 ml) Creamy Garlic
Sauce (page 114)

1 teaspoon finely chopped fresh
rosemary, plus 1 tablespoon
rosemary leaves

Semolina flour, for dusting

One 9-oz (250-g) ball NY Style
Pizza Dough (page 98)

**MAKES ONE 12-INCH (30-CM)
PIZZA; SERVES 2–4**

Position an oven rack in the middle of the oven and place a pizza
stone on the rack. Preheat the oven to 550°F/290°C (or as high
as it will go). Once the oven has reached 550°F/290°C, let the
stone continue to heat for 15–30 minutes longer, without opening
the door.

In a medium bowl, combine the water and salt, stirring until
dissolved. Add the potato slices and let soak for 15 minutes.
Drain and blot the potato slices dry. Transfer to another medium
bowl, then toss the potato slices with the olive oil and season
with salt and pepper.

In a small bowl, stir together the sauce and chopped rosemary.

On a lightly floured surface, stretch the pizza dough into a 12-inch
(30-cm) round. If the dough springs back, let it rest for about
10 minutes before continuing. Dust a pizza peel with semolina
and transfer the dough round to the pizza peel.

Brush the edge of the dough round with olive oil. Leaving a 1-inch
(2.5-cm) border, spread the sauce over the dough and arrange
the potato slices on top.

Carefully slide the pizza from the peel onto the hot stone in the
oven and bake for about 8 minutes, or until the crust is golden
brown. Using the peel, transfer the pizza to a cutting board.
Sprinkle with the rosemary leaves and a few grinds of pepper.
Let cool for about 1 minute, then slice and serve right away.

QUATTRO FORMAGGI PIZZA

"Quattro formaggi" pizza is a simple but traditional pizza—although which four cheeses you use is up to you. Most versions include the standard mozzarella, Parmesan, and ricotta. This recipe adds Gorgonzola as the fourth; if you don't like blue cheese, swap it out for fontina, smoked mozzarella, or pecorino.

One 6-oz (170-g) ball fresh mozzarella cheese, preferably buffalo, thinly sliced

Semolina flour, for dusting

One 9-oz (250-g) ball NY Style Pizza Dough (page 98) or Whole Wheat Pizza Dough (page 96)

Extra-virgin olive oil, for brushing and drizzling

1/3–1/2 cup (80–120 ml) All-Purpose Pizza Sauce (page 106)

1/3 cup (45 g) crumbled Gorgonzola cheese

1/4 cup (30 g) grated Parmesan cheese

1/4 cup (60 g) whole-milk ricotta cheese

4–6 fresh basil leaves, torn into big pieces

MAKES ONE 12-INCH (30-CM) PIZZA; SERVES 2–4

Position an oven rack in the middle of the oven and place a pizza stone on the rack. Preheat the oven to 550°F/290°C (or as high as it will go). Once the oven has reached 550°F/290°C, let the stone continue to heat for 15–30 minutes longer, without opening the door.

If using buffalo mozzarella, spread the pieces on paper towels and blot dry slightly. Set aside.

On a lightly floured surface, stretch the pizza dough into a 12-inch (30-cm) round. If the dough springs back, let it rest for about 10 minutes before continuing. Dust a pizza peel with semolina and transfer the dough round to the pizza peel.

Brush the edge of the dough round with olive oil. Leaving a 1-inch (2.5-cm) border, spread the sauce over the dough and top with the mozzarella, then the Gorgonzola, and then the Parmesan. Finally, dollop with the ricotta.

Carefully slide the pizza from the peel onto the hot stone in the oven and bake for about 8 minutes, or until the crust is golden brown. Using the peel, transfer the pizza to a cutting board. Drizzle with olive oil. Let cool for about 1 minute, then scatter the basil over the top, slice, and serve right away.

MARGHERITA PIZZA

The original pizza from Naples, this is the one that all others are measured by. Because of its simplicity, it really is the sum of its parts. For best results, be sure to blot slices of buffalo mozzarella as dry as possible.

One 6–8 oz (170–225 g) ball fresh mozzarella cheese, preferably buffalo, sliced and torn into pieces

Semolina flour, for dusting

One 9-oz (250-g) ball NY Style Pizza Dough (page 98)

Extra-virgin olive oil, for brushing and drizzling

⅓–½ cup (80–120 ml) All-Purpose Pizza Sauce (page 106)

Fresh basil leaves, for garnish

MAKES ONE 12-INCH (30-CM) PIZZA; SERVES 2–4

Position an oven rack in the middle of the oven and place a pizza stone on the rack. Preheat the oven to 550°F/290°C (or as high as it will go). Once the oven has reached 550°F/290°C, let the stone continue to heat for 15–30 minutes longer, without opening the door.

If using buffalo mozzarella, spread the pieces on paper towels and blot dry slightly. Set aside.

On a lightly floured surface, stretch the pizza dough into a 12-inch (30-cm) round or oval. If the dough springs back, let it rest for about 10 minutes before continuing. Dust a pizza peel with semolina and transfer the dough round to the pizza peel.

Brush the edge of the dough round with olive oil. Leaving a 1-inch (2.5-cm) border, spread the sauce over the dough and top with the cheese.

Carefully slide the pizza from the peel onto the hot stone in the oven and bake for about 8 minutes, or until the crust is golden brown. Using the peel, transfer the pizza to a cutting board. Drizzle with olive oil. Let cool for about 1 minute, then scatter basil over the top, slice, and serve right away.

ASPARAGUS & GOAT CHEESE PIZZA WITH RED PEPPER PESTO

Roasted red pepper pesto is an easy way to add flair to this vegetarian pizza. When asparagus isn't in season, try other vegetables, like roasted or grilled eggplant, chopped baby spinach, or cherry tomatoes.

½ lb (225 g) asparagus, tough woody ends removed

2 teaspoons extra-virgin olive oil, plus more for brushing and drizzling

Kosher salt and freshly ground pepper

Semolina flour, for dusting

One 9-oz (250-g) ball NY Style Pizza Dough (page 98) or Whole Wheat Pizza Dough (page 96)

⅓ cup (80 ml) Roasted Red Pepper Pesto (page 110)

¾ cup (90 g) shredded low-moisture mozzarella cheese

4 oz (90 g) crumbled goat cheese

MAKES ONE 12-INCH (30-CM) PIZZA; SERVES 2–4

Position an oven rack in the middle of the oven and place a pizza stone on the rack. Preheat the oven to 550°F/290°C (or as high as it will go). Once the oven has reached 550°F/290°C, let the stone continue to heat for 15–30 minutes longer, without opening the door.

Bring a saucepan of water to a boil over high heat. Add the asparagus and cook for about 1 minute, or just until crisp-tender. Drain and transfer to a medium bowl, then toss with the olive oil and season with salt and pepper.

On a lightly floured surface, stretch the pizza dough into a 12-inch (30-cm) round. If the dough springs back, let it rest for about 10 minutes before continuing. Dust a pizza peel with semolina and transfer the dough round to the pizza peel.

Brush the edge of the dough round with olive oil. Leaving a 1-inch (2.5-cm) border, spread the pesto over the dough and top with the mozzarella. Distribute the goat cheese on the pizza. Arrange the asparagus spears horizontally with the dough.

Carefully slide the pizza from the peel onto the hot stone in the oven and bake for about 8 minutes, or until the crust is golden brown. Using the peel, transfer the pizza to a cutting board. Drizzle with olive oil. Let cool for about 1 minute, then slice and serve right away.

WILD MUSHROOM, CARAMELIZED ONION & FONTINA PIZZA

This elegant pizza combines earthy mushrooms, sweet onions, and nutty fontina with a garlic-infused white sauce, creating a meal worthy of a dinner party. Add a light layer of chopped sautéed greens to the pie if you like.

2 tablespoons extra-virgin olive oil, plus more for brushing

½ yellow onion, thinly sliced

5 oz (140 g) wild mushrooms, such as cremini, shiitake, porcini, or oyster, or a mixture, brushed clean

2 cloves garlic, minced

Kosher salt and freshly ground pepper

Semolina flour, for dusting

One 9-oz (250-g) ball NY Style Pizza Dough (page 98) or Whole Wheat Pizza Dough (page 96)

⅓ cup (80 ml) Creamy Garlic Sauce (page 114) or All-Purpose Pizza Sauce (page 106)

1 cup (115 g) shredded fontina cheese or low-moisture mozzarella cheese

MAKES ONE 12-INCH (30-CM) PIZZA; SERVES 2–4

Position an oven rack in the middle of the oven and place a pizza stone on the rack. Preheat the oven to 550°F/290°C (or as high as it will go). Once the oven has reached 550°F/290°C, let the stone continue to heat for 15–30 minutes longer, without opening the door.

In a frying pan over low heat, warm 1 tablespoon of the olive oil. Add the onion and cook, stirring occasionally, for about 20 minutes, or until tender and golden.

In the same pan over medium-high heat, warm the remaining 1 tablespoon oil. Add the mushrooms and garlic, season with salt and pepper, and cook, stirring occasionally, for about 4 minutes, or until the mushrooms soften.Remove from the heat and set aside.

On a lightly floured surface, stretch the pizza dough into a 12-inch (30-cm) round. If the dough springs back, let it rest for about 10 minutes before continuing. Dust a pizza peel with semolina and transfer the dough round to the pizza peel.

Brush the edge of the dough round with olive oil. Leaving a 1-inch (2.5-cm) border, spread the sauce over the dough. Arrange the caramelized onion over the sauce and top with the cheese. Distribute the mushroom mixture over the pizza.

Carefully slide the pizza from the peel onto the hot stone in the oven and bake for about 8 minutes, or until the crust is golden brown. Using the peel, transfer the pizza to a cutting board. Let cool for about 1 minute, then slice and serve right away.

EGGPLANT PARMESAN
SHEET PAN PIZZA

If you love eggplant Parmesan, then this pizza is for you. Salting the eggplant removes the bitterness, so don't skip this step. A scattering of basil adds freshness to this family-favorite sheet pan pizza.

Sheet Pan Pizza Dough (page 102), partially baked

1 lb (450 g) Italian eggplant, cut into ½-inch (12-mm) cubes

1 teaspoon kosher salt

2 tablespoons extra-virgin olive oil, plus more for brushing

¾ cup (180 ml) All-Purpose Pizza Sauce (page 106)

1½ cups (170 g) shredded low-moisture mozzarella cheese

½ cup (60 g) grated Parmesan cheese

¼ cup (15 g) shredded fresh basil

MAKES 1 LARGE SHEET PAN PIZZA; SERVES 6

If the partially baked dough was frozen, let thaw completely and come to room temperature.

Put the eggplant cubes in a colander set in the sink or a large bowl and toss with the salt. Set aside for 30 minutes.

Position 2 oven racks in the middle and in the upper third of the oven and preheat to 450°F/230°C.

Spread the eggplant on a baking sheet and blot dry. Drizzle with the olive oil and toss to coat. Spread the eggplant in a single layer. Roast on the middle rack, stirring once about halfway through, for about 20 minutes, or until tender and golden brown. Remove from the oven and set aside.

Brush the dough lightly with olive oil. Leaving a ½-inch (12-mm) border, spread the sauce over the dough. Top with the eggplant, mozzarella, and Parmesan cheese, distributing them evenly over the pizza.

Bake the pizza on the upper rack for about 18 minutes, or until the crust is golden brown. Slide the pizza off the baking sheet and onto a cutting board. Scatter the basil over the top. Let cool for a few minutes, then slice and serve right away.

THREE CHEESE STROMBOLI WITH PESTO & ROASTED PEPPERS

Stromboli is like a pinwheel pizza (as opposed to a calzone, which is similar to a stuffed turnover). It's a great choice for a party because it can be made ahead and filled with a variety of ingredients. This recipe is a good starting point. Other filling combos include Italian salami, prosciutto, and provolone; pepperoni, mozzarella, and olives; or spinach, mushrooms, and feta.

Semolina flour, for dusting

One 9-oz (250-g) ball NY Style Pizza Dough (page 98) or Whole Wheat Pizza Dough (page 96)

½ cup (120 ml) Classic Basil Pesto (page 109)

¼ cup (40 g) chopped jarred roasted red bell pepper, drained

1 cup (115 g) shredded low-moisture mozzarella cheese

½ cup (115 g) whole-milk ricotta cheese

¼ cup (30 g) grated Parmesan cheese

Kosher salt and freshly ground pepper

1 large egg, beaten with 1 teaspoon water, for egg wash

MAKES 2–4 SERVINGS

Position an oven rack in the middle of the oven and place a pizza stone on the rack. Preheat the oven to 550°F/290°C (or as high as it will go). Once the oven has reached 550°F/290°C, let the stone continue to heat for 15–30 minutes longer, without opening the door.

On a lightly floured surface, stretch the pizza dough into a 10-by-14-inch (25-by-35-cm) rectangle. If the dough springs back, let it rest for about 10 minutes before continuing.

With a long side facing you, spread the pesto over the dough, leaving a 1-inch (2.5-cm) border on each short side and a 3-inch (7.5-cm) border on the long side farthest away from you. Scatter the roasted pepper over the pesto. In a bowl, stir together the mozzarella, ricotta, and Parmesan, and season with salt and pepper. Dollop the cheese mixture all over the pesto and roasted peppers.

Using a pastry brush, brush some egg wash on the uncovered edges of the dough. Fold over the 2 short sides to the 1-inch (2.5-cm) mark and brush the tops with egg wash. Keeping the short sides tucked in, tightly roll up the stromboli lengthwise away from you.

Dust a pizza peel with semolina. Crimp the seams tightly to seal and transfer the stromboli, seam side down, onto the peel. Brush the stromboli all over with the egg wash. Using the tip of a sharp knife, make a few slits along the top of the dough, about 2 inches (5 cm) apart.

Carefully slide the stromboli from the peel onto the hot stone in the oven, keeping it seam side down. Bake for about 10 minutes, or until the crust is golden brown and cooked throughout. Using the peel, transfer the stromboli to a cutting board and let rest for 5 minutes. Carefully cut crosswise into slices and serve right away.

DEEP DISH MUSHROOM, ARTICHOKE & SPINACH PIE WITH RICOTTA

Baked in a cast–iron pan, this one–dish meal has it all, with a thick cornmeal crust stuffed with creamy ricotta and plenty of veggies. Be sure to drain any excess liquid from the cooked mushrooms and spinach to prevent a soggy bottom.

4 tablespoons (60 ml) extra-virgin olive oil, plus more for brushing

½ small red onion, thinly sliced

Kosher salt and freshly ground pepper

8 oz (225 g) cremini or button mushrooms, brushed clean and thickly sliced

5 oz (140 g) baby spinach

One ball Deep Dish Cornmeal Pizza Dough (page 103)

6 oz (170 g) quartered marinated artichoke hearts, drained and roughly chopped

½ cup (115 g) whole–milk ricotta cheese

1 cup (240 ml) All-Purpose Pizza Sauce (page 106)

1 cup (115 g) shredded low-moisture mozzarella cheese

¼ cup (30 g) grated Parmesan cheese

MAKES ONE 10-INCH (25-CM) DEEP DISH PIZZA; SERVES 4–6

Position an oven rack in the lower third of the oven and preheat to 400°F/200°C.

In a large frying pan over medium heat, warm 1 tablespoon of the olive oil. Add the onion and season with salt and pepper. Cook, stirring occasionally, for about 3 minutes, or until the onion is soft and beginning to brown. Transfer to a large plate.

In the same pan over medium heat, warm 2 tablespoons of the olive oil. Add the mushrooms and season with salt and pepper. Cook, stirring a few times, for 5–6 minutes, or until the mushrooms soften and begin to brown. Transfer to the plate with the onion.

Add the remaining 1 tablespoon olive oil and the spinach to the pan. Season with salt and pepper and cook, stirring, for about 4 minutes, or until the spinach wilts. Transfer to the plate with the onion and mushrooms.

Brush a 10-inch (25-cm) cast–iron frying pan with olive oil. Put the pizza dough in the pan and pat into a disk. Using your hands, press the dough into the pan, nudging it gently into an even layer on the bottom and halfway up the sides. Brush the dough with more olive oil and top with the onion, mushrooms, spinach, and artichoke hearts. Dollop the ricotta all over the top. Pour the sauce over the top and gently spread it out. Sprinkle with the mozzarella and then the Parmesan.

Bake for about 35 minutes, or until the bottom of the dough is nicely browned (lift with a spatula or long-bladed knife to peek). Remove from the oven and let cool for 5 minutes. Slice the pizza directly in the pan and serve right away.

EGGPLANT & BLACK OLIVE CALZONES WITH SPICY ARRABIATA SAUCE

Once you get the hang of assembling calzones—oven-baked pizza turnovers—you'll discover their endless versatility. They can be stuffed with any combination of veggies, meats, sauce, and cheese. Calzones are delicious right out the oven, but they also freeze well after baking. Let thaw at room temperature, then warm in a 350°F/180°C oven.

1 lb (450 g) Italian eggplant, diced

1 teaspoon kosher salt

2 tablespoons extra-virgin olive oil

Freshly ground pepper

Two 9-oz (250-g) balls NY Style Pizza Dough (page 98)

Semolina flour, for dusting

1 large egg, beaten with 1 teaspoon water, for egg wash

8 tablespoons (120 ml) Spicy Arrabiata Sauce (page 111), plus more for serving

8 tablespoons (70 g) pitted and sliced black olives, such as Kalamata

8 tablespoons (60 g) shredded low-moisture mozzarella cheese

4 tablespoons (30 g) grated Parmesan cheese

MAKES 4 CALZONES

Put the eggplant cubes in a colander set in the sink or a large bowl and toss with the salt. Set aside for 30 minutes.

Position 2 oven racks in the middle and in the lower third of the oven and preheat to 450°F/230°C. Place a pizza stone on the lower rack.

Spread the eggplant on a baking sheet and blot dry. Drizzle with the olive oil and toss to coat. Spread in a single layer and season with pepper. Roast on the middle rack, stirring once halfway through, for about 20 minutes, or until tender and golden brown. Remove from the oven and set aside.

Move the pizza stone to the middle rack and raise the oven temperature to 550°F/290°C (or as high as it will go).

Divide the pizza dough into 4 equal pieces. On a lightly floured surface, stretch each piece into an 8-inch (20-cm) round. Brush half of each dough round with some of the egg wash. Leaving a ½-inch (12-mm) border, top one-half of each dough round with 2 tablespoons of the sauce; one-fourth of the eggplant; 2 tablespoons of the olives; 2 tablespoons of the mozzarella, and 1 tablespoon of the Parmesan.

Fold the uncovered half of each calzone up and over the filling to meet the opposite edges, then crimp the edges of the dough tightly to seal. Brush the tops of the calzones with egg wash. Using the tip of a sharp knife, make a slit in the top of each calzone.

Dust a pizza peel with semolina and transfer a calzone to the peel. Carefully slide the calzone from the peel onto the hot stone in the oven. Repeat with the remaining calzones, spacing them evenly on the stone. Bake for about 8 minutes, or until the crusts are golden brown. Using the peel, transfer the calzones to a cutting board or wire rack and let cool for 5 minutes, then serve right away with sauce on the side for dipping.

MEAT &
SEAFOOD
PIZZAS

PEACH, PROSCIUTTO & PESTO PIZZA

The combination of sweet, salty, peppery, and earthy are well-balanced in this summery pizza topped with fresh peaches, a swath of basil pesto, baby arugula, and tender prosciutto. If you like, swap out nectarines for the peaches, but be sure to use sweet ripe fruit at the height of summer.

Semolina flour, for dusting

One 9-oz (250-g) ball NY Style Pizza Dough (page 98)

Extra-virgin olive oil, for brushing

⅓ cup (80 ml) Classic Basil Pesto (page 109)

1 ripe peach, halved, pitted, and thinly sliced

Kosher salt and freshly ground pepper

2 oz (60 g) thinly sliced prosciutto

¼ cup (30 g) grated Parmesan cheese

½ cup (15 g) baby arugula

Aged balsamic vinegar, for drizzling

MAKES ONE 12-INCH (30-CM) PIZZA; SERVES 2–4

Position an oven rack in the middle of the oven and place a pizza stone on the rack. Preheat the oven to 550°F/290°C (or as high as it will go). Once the oven has reached 550°F/290°C, let the stone continue to heat for 15–30 minutes longer, without opening the door.

On a lightly floured surface, stretch the pizza dough into a 12-inch (30-cm) round. If the dough springs back, let it rest for about 10 minutes before continuing. Dust a pizza peel with semolina and transfer the dough round to the pizza peel.

Brush the edge of the dough round with olive oil. Leaving a 1-inch (2.5-cm) border, spread the pesto evenly over the dough. Arrange the peach slices on top, season with salt and pepper, and drape the prosciutto among the peaches.

Carefully slide the pizza from the peel onto the hot stone in the oven and bake for about 8 minutes, or until the crust is golden brown. Using the peel, transfer the pizza to a cutting board. Sprinkle with the cheese, top with the arugula, and drizzle with a little vinegar. Let cool for about 1 minute, then slice and serve right away.

CARAMELIZED PINEAPPLE & SMOKED HAM PIZZA

Love it or hate it, pineapple and ham pizza is here to stay. For those who are fans, this version takes it one step further with deliciously caramelized pineapple. Be sure to use fresh fruit for the best result.

1 tablespoon unsalted butter

1 teaspoon sugar

Two ½-inch-thick (12-mm) slices fresh peeled and cored pineapple

Semolina flour, for dusting

One 9-oz (250-g) ball NY Style Pizza Dough (page 98) or Whole Wheat Pizza Dough (page 96)

Extra-virgin olive oil, for brushing

⅓–½ cup (80–120 ml) All-Purpose Pizza Sauce (page 106)

1 cup (115 g) shredded low-moisture mozzarella cheese

One 3-oz (90-g) slice smoked ham, chopped

MAKES ONE 12-INCH (30-CM) PIZZA; SERVES 2–4

Position an oven rack in the middle of the oven and place a pizza stone on the rack. Preheat the oven to 550°F/290°C (or as high as it will go). Once the oven has reached 550°F/290°C, let the stone continue to heat for 15–30 minutes longer, without opening the door.

In a frying pan over medium-high heat, melt the butter. Sprinkle the sugar over the butter and allow the butter to brown slightly. Add the pineapple slices and cook, turning once, for about 5 minutes per side, or until they caramelize. Transfer to a plate and let cool, then chop into ½-inch (12-mm) dice.

On a lightly floured surface, stretch the pizza dough into a 12-inch (30-cm) round. If the dough springs back, let it rest for about 10 minutes before continuing. Dust a pizza peel with semolina and transfer the dough round to the pizza peel.

Brush the edge of the dough round with olive oil. Leaving a 1-inch (2.5-cm) border, spread the sauce over the dough and top with the cheese. Distribute the pineapple and the ham over the pizza.

Carefully slide the pizza from the peel onto the hot stone in the oven and bake for about 8 minutes, or until the crust is golden brown. Using the peel, transfer the pizza to a cutting board. Let cool for about 1 minute, then slice and serve right away.

MEATBALL PIZZA

Mini meatballs top this much-loved East Coast classic, and if you make a double batch of the meatballs, you can throw this pie together in no time on a busy weeknight. The meatballs freeze well; just thaw them at room temperature for a few hours before topping your pizza.

¼ small red onion, thinly sliced

1 teaspoon balsamic vinegar

Extra-virgin olive oil, for drizzling, greasing, and brushing

Kosher salt and freshly ground pepper

¼ lb (115 g) sweet Italian sausage, casings removed

¼ lb (115 g) ground beef

4 tablespoons (30 g) grated Parmesan cheese

Semolina flour, for dusting

Two 9-oz (250-g) balls NY Style Pizza Dough (page 98)

⅓–½ cup (80–120 ml) All-Purpose Pizza Sauce (page 106)

1 cup (115 g) shredded low-moisture mozzarella cheese

MAKES ONE 12-INCH (30-CM) PIZZA; SERVES 2–4

Position an oven rack in the middle of the oven and place a pizza stone on the rack. Preheat the oven to 550°F/290°C (or as high as it will go). Once the oven has reached 550°F/290°C, let the stone continue to heat for 15–30 minutes longer, without opening the door.

In a small bowl, toss the onion with the vinegar, drizzle with olive oil, and season with salt and pepper. Set aside.

Grease a small rimmed baking sheet with olive oil. In a medium bowl, combine the sausage, beef, and 2 tablespoons of the Parmesan. Season lightly with salt and pepper and mix gently with your hands. Using 1 teaspoon of the meat mixture for each, form into mini meatballs and place on the prepared baking sheet. Transfer the baking sheet to the hot pizza stone and bake for about 6 minutes, or until browned. Set aside.

On a lightly floured surface, stretch the pizza dough into a 12-inch (30-cm) round or oval. If the dough springs back, let it rest for about 10 minutes before continuing. Dust a pizza peel with semolina and transfer the dough round to the pizza peel.

Brush the edge of the dough round with olive oil. Leaving a 1-inch (2.5-cm) border, spread the sauce over the dough and top with the mozzarella and the remaining 2 tablespoons Parmesan. Distribute the meatballs over the pizza, gently pushing them in place so they don't slide around, then scatter the marinated onions on top.

Carefully slide the pizza from the peel onto the hot stone in the oven and bake for about 8 minutes, or until the crust is golden brown. Using the peel, transfer the pizza to a cutting board. Let cool for about 1 minute, then slice and serve right away.

BURGER NIGHT PIZZA

Topped with seasoned ground beef, a blend of mozzarella and Cheddar cheese, and sliced dill pickles, this pizza might just be your new favorite mash-up meal. For a more burger-like base, try these toppings on the Sheet Pan Pizza Dough (page 102).

2 tablespoons extra-virgin olive oil, plus more for brushing

½ yellow onion, thinly sliced

2 cloves garlic, minced

¾ lb (340 g) ground beef

Kosher salt and freshly ground pepper

Semolina flour, for dusting

One 9-oz (250-g) ball NY Style Pizza Dough (page 98)

½ cup (120 ml) All-Purpose Pizza Sauce (page 106)

½ cup (60 g) shredded low-moisture mozzarella cheese

½ cup (60 g) shredded Cheddar cheese

¼ cup (40 g) sliced dill pickles (optional)

MAKES ONE 12-INCH (30-CM) PIZZA; SERVES 2–4

Position an oven rack in the middle of the oven and place a pizza stone on the rack. Preheat the oven to 550°F/290°C (or as high as it will go). Once the oven has reached 550°F/290°C, let the stone continue to heat for 15–30 minutes longer, without opening the door.

In a frying pan over low heat, warm 1 tablespoon of the olive oil. Add the onion and cook, stirring occasionally, for about 20 minutes, or until tender and golden. Transfer the onion to a bowl.

In the same pan over medium-high heat, warm the remaining 1 tablespoon olive oil. Add the garlic and cook, stirring occasionally, for about 1 minute, or until it just begins to soften but not brown. Add the ground beef and season with salt and pepper. Cook, stirring occasionally and using your spoon to break up any clumps, for about 5 minutes, or until the meat is browned. Using a slotted spoon, transfer the beef to another bowl.

On a lightly floured surface, stretch the pizza dough into a 12-inch (30-cm) round. If the dough springs back, let it rest for about 10 minutes before continuing. Dust a pizza peel with semolina and transfer the dough round to the pizza peel.

Brush the edge of the dough round with olive oil. Leaving a 1-inch (2.5-cm) border, spread the sauce over the dough round and top with the ground beef and caramelized onion. Sprinkle with the mozzarella and Cheddar. Arrange the dill pickles, if using, over the top of the pizza.

Carefully slide the pizza from the peel onto the hot stone in the oven and bake for about 8 minutes, or until the crust is golden brown. Using the peel, transfer the pizza to a cutting board. Let cool for about 1 minute, then slice and serve right away.

SOPPRESSATA, ROASTED PEPPER & BUFFALO MOZZARELLA PIZZA

An Italian dry salami, soppressata makes an excellent addition to pizza. If you like, swap out the tomato sauce for Roasted Red Pepper Pesto (page 110) and omit the additional roasted peppers. Serve this with a medium-bodied Italian red wine and the Antipasti Salad with Peperoncini Vinaigrette (page 84).

One 6–8 oz (170–225 g) ball fresh mozzarella cheese, preferably buffalo, sliced and torn into pieces

Semolina flour, for dusting

One 9-oz (250-g) ball NY Style Pizza Dough (page 98) or Whole Wheat Pizza Dough (page 96)

Extra-virgin olive oil, for brushing

⅓–½ cup (80–120 ml) All-Purpose Pizza Sauce (page 106)

¼ cup (30 g) grated Parmesan cheese

3 oz (90 g) soppressata, thinly sliced

¼ cup (40 g) chopped jarred roasted red bell peppers, drained

8 fresh basil leaves, torn into large pieces

MAKES ONE 12-INCH (30-CM) PIZZA; SERVES 2–4

Position an oven rack in the middle of the oven and place a pizza stone on the rack. Preheat the oven to 550°F/290°C (or as high as it will go). Once the oven has reached 550°F/290°C, let the stone continue to heat for 15–30 minutes longer, without opening the door.

If using buffalo mozzarella, spread the pieces on paper towels and blot dry slightly. Set aside.

On a lightly floured surface, stretch the pizza dough into a 12-inch (30-cm) round. If the dough springs back, let it rest for about 10 minutes before continuing. Dust a pizza peel with semolina and transfer the dough round to the pizza peel.

Brush the edge of the dough round with olive oil. Leaving a 1-inch (2.5-cm) border, spread the sauce over the dough and top with the mozzarella and Parmesan. Arrange the soppressata over the pizza, then sprinkle with the roasted peppers.

Carefully slide the pizza from the peel onto the hot stone in the oven and bake for about 8 minutes, or until the crust is golden brown. Using the peel, transfer the pizza to a cutting board. Let cool for about 1 minute, then sprinkle with the basil, slice, and serve right away.

SPANISH CHORIZO, MANCHEGO & OREGANO PIZZA

Spanish chorizo is a cured meat, similar to salami, and made with plenty of spices, including lots of smoked paprika. This pizza celebrates the best of Spain with a layer of romesco sauce, a sprinkling of Spanish Manchego cheese, and drizzles of oregano oil.

1 tablespoon extra-virgin olive oil

1 teaspoon dried oregano

Kosher salt and freshly ground pepper

Semolina flour, for dusting

One 9-oz (250-g) ball NY Style Pizza Dough (page 98)

½ cup (120 ml) store-bought romesco sauce or All-Purpose Pizza Sauce (page 106)

3 oz (90 g) shaved Manchego cheese

½ cup (60 g) shredded low-moisture mozzarella cheese

¼ lb (115 g) cured Spanish-style chorizo, cut on the diagonal into ¼-inch (6-mm) slices

MAKES ONE 12-INCH (30-CM) PIZZA; SERVES 2–4

Position an oven rack in the middle of the oven and place a pizza stone on the rack. Preheat the oven to 550°F/290°C (or as high as it will go). Once the oven has reached 550°F/290°C, let the stone continue to heat for 15–30 minutes longer, without opening the door.

In a small bowl, stir together the olive oil and oregano and season with salt and pepper. Set aside.

On a lightly floured surface, stretch the pizza dough into a 12-inch (30-cm) round. If the dough springs back, let it rest for about 10 minutes before continuing. Dust a pizza peel with semolina and transfer the dough round to the pizza peel.

Leaving a 1-inch (2.5-cm) border, spread the sauce over the dough. Sprinkle with the Manchego and mozzarella, then arrange the chorizo in a single layer on top. Drizzle with the oregano oil.

Carefully slide the pizza from the peel onto the hot stone in the oven and bake for about 8 minutes, or until the crust is golden brown. Using the peel, transfer the pizza to a cutting board. Let cool for about 1 minute, then slice and serve right away.

KALE SALAD PIADINE WITH BACON, PARMESAN & LEMON ZEST

A piadina is an Italian flatbread often folded over a variety of ingredients to create a sandwich. Here, a thin pizza crust is first brushed with garlic oil, then baked and topped with a distinctive lemon-kissed kale, bacon, and Parmesan salad that explodes with flavor.

3 tablespoons extra-virgin olive oil

2 large cloves garlic, minced

1 large bunch lacinato kale

Kosher salt and freshly ground pepper

1 teaspoon grated lemon zest

4 slices thick-cut applewood-smoked bacon, chopped

¼ cup (30 g) grated Parmesan cheese

Two 9-oz (250-g) balls NY Style Pizza Dough (page 98) or Whole Wheat Pizza Dough (page 96)

Semolina flour, for dusting

1 tablespoon balsamic vinegar, or to taste

1 teaspoon fresh lemon juice, or to taste

MAKES FOUR 8-INCH (20-CM) PIADINE; SERVES 4

Position an oven rack in the middle of the oven and place a pizza stone on the rack. Preheat the oven to 550°F/290°C (or as high as it will go). Once the oven has reached 550°F/290°C, let the stone continue to heat for 15–30 minutes longer, without opening the door.

In a frying pan over low heat, combine the olive oil and garlic and cook, stirring occasionally, for about 1 minute, or just until the garlic is fragrant. Strain the oil through a fine-mesh sieve into a small bowl, discarding the garlic. Let cool completely.

Using your hands, strip the ribs from the kale. Roll the leaves up and thinly slice them crosswise, then coarsely chop. Place the kale in a large bowl, sprinkle with salt and the lemon zest, and massage the leaves to soften them.

In the same frying pan over medium heat, fry the bacon, stirring, for about 5 minutes, or until crisp. Transfer to paper towels to drain, then add the bacon and the Parmesan to the bowl with the kale. Toss to combine. Set aside.

To make the piadine, divide the pizza dough into 4 equal pieces. On a lightly floured surface, stretch each piece into an 8-inch (20-cm) round. If the dough springs back, let it rest for about 10 minutes before continuing. Brush each dough round with the garlic oil, reserving 1 tablespoon for the salad, and season with salt and pepper.

Dust a pizza peel with semolina and transfer a dough round to the pizza peel. Carefully slide a piadina from the peel onto the hot stone in the oven and bake for 4–6 minutes, or until golden brown. Using the peel, transfer to a plate. Repeat with the remaining piadine.

Drizzle the salad with the reserved garlic oil, the vinegar, and lemon juice. Season with salt and pepper. Toss to combine. Divide the salad among the piadine and serve right away.

BRUSSELS SPROUTS & BACON PIZZA

The robust flavor of Brussels sprouts is nicely balanced by the addition of smoky bacon and sweet balsamic vinegar in this pizza. Shaving the sprouts ensures they will cook until tender and even get a little caramelization from the heat of the oven.

One 8-oz (225-g) ball fresh mozzarella cheese, preferably buffalo, diced

3 slices thick-cut applewood-smoked bacon, chopped

¾ cup (60 g) Brussels sprouts, halved and cored, outer leaves kept whole and the rest thinly sliced or shaved

½ small red onion, thinly sliced

Kosher salt and freshly ground pepper

1½ teaspoons balsamic vinegar

Semolina flour, for dusting

One 9-oz (250-g) ball NY Style Pizza Dough (page 98) or Whole Wheat Pizza Dough (page 96)

Extra-virgin olive oil, for brushing

⅓–½ cup (80–120 ml) All-Purpose Pizza Sauce (page 106)

MAKES ONE 12-INCH (30-CM) PIZZA; SERVES 2–4

Position an oven rack in the middle of the oven and place a pizza stone on the rack. Preheat the oven to 550°F/290°C (or as high as it will go). Once the oven has reached 550°F/290°C, let the stone continue to heat for 15–30 minutes longer, without opening the door.

If using buffalo mozzarella, spread the pieces on paper towels and blot dry slightly. Set aside.

In a large frying pan over medium heat, fry the bacon, stirring, for about 6 minutes, or until crisp. Transfer to paper towels to drain.

Pour off all but 1 tablespoon of the fat from the pan and return the pan to medium-high heat. Add the Brussels sprouts and onion, season with salt and pepper, and cook, stirring occasionally, for about 5 minutes, or until the vegetables soften and begin to brown. Stir in the vinegar and sauté until the liquid is absorbed, about 2 minutes. Remove from the heat and set aside.

On a lightly floured surface, stretch the pizza dough into a 12-inch (30-cm) round or oval. If the dough springs back, let it rest for about 10 minutes before continuing. Dust a pizza peel with semolina and transfer the dough round to the pizza peel.

Brush the edge of the dough round with olive oil. Leaving a 1-inch (2.5-cm) border, spread the sauce over the dough and top with the cheese. Distribute the Brussels sprouts and onion and the bacon over the pizza.

Carefully slide the pizza from the peel onto the hot stone in the oven and bake for about 8 minutes, or until the crust is golden brown. Using the peel, transfer the pizza to a cutting board. Let cool for about 1 minute, then slice and serve right away.

SAUSAGE, SHAVED FENNEL & FRESH TOMATO PIZZA

Classic sausage pizza gets a lift from fresh ripe tomatoes and crunchy shaved fennel. For an extra boost of fennel flavor, look for Italian sausage that includes fennel seeds. Plum tomatoes work well because they aren't overly watery, but when heirlooms are at their seasonal peak, they make an exceptional substitute.

1 tablespoon extra-virgin olive oil, plus more for brushing

½ cup (50 g) very thinly sliced fresh fennel

½ lb (225 g) sweet or spicy Italian sausage, casings removed

Semolina flour, for dusting

One 9-oz (250-g) ball NY Style Pizza Dough (page 98) or Whole Wheat Pizza Dough (page 96)

1 cup (115 g) shredded low-moisture mozzarella cheese

3 ripe plum tomatoes, thinly sliced

1 teaspoon finely chopped fresh rosemary

MAKES ONE 12-INCH (30-CM) PIZZA; SERVES 2–4

Position an oven rack in the middle of the oven and place a pizza stone on the rack. Preheat the oven to 550°F/290°C (or as high as it will go). Once the oven has reached 550°F/290°C, let the stone continue to heat for 15–30 minutes longer, without opening the door.

In a frying pan over medium-high heat, warm the olive oil. Add the fennel and cook, stirring occasionally, for about 3 minutes, or until lightly browned. Transfer to a plate. Add the sausage to the pan and cook, stirring occasionally, using your spoon to break up any clumps, for about 5 minutes, or until cooked through. Using a slotted spoon, transfer to paper towels to drain.

On a lightly floured surface, stretch the pizza dough into a 12-inch (30-cm) round. If the dough springs back, let it rest for about 10 minutes before continuing. Dust a pizza peel with semolina and transfer the dough round to the pizza peel.

Brush the edge of the dough round with olive oil. Leaving a 1-inch (2.5-cm) border, cover the dough round with the mozzarella and arrange the tomato slices on top. Distribute the sausage around the pizza, breaking it up with your fingers as needed, then scatter the fennel and rosemary over the top.

Carefully slide the pizza from the peel onto the hot stone in the oven and bake for about 8 minutes, or until the crust is golden brown. Using the peel, transfer the pizza to a cutting board. Let cool for about 1 minute, then slice and serve right away.

CHORIZO, POTATO & SPINACH PIZZA

Mexican chorizo is a fresh, spicy sausage made from pork; it's different than cured Spanish chorizo, which is dried. You can substitute hot Italian sausage here if you like, but the chorizo and potatoes are a classic pairing that's not to be missed.

1 Yukon gold potato, peeled and diced

1 tablespoon extra-virgin olive oil, plus more for brushing

2 cloves garlic, minced

8 oz (225 g) baby spinach

Kosher salt and freshly ground pepper

⅓ lb (140 g) fresh Mexican-style chorizo, casings removed

Semolina flour, for dusting

One 9-oz (250-g) ball NY Style Pizza Dough (page 98) or Whole Wheat Pizza Dough (page 96)

⅓–½ cup (80–120 ml) All-Purpose Pizza Sauce (page 106)

1 cup (115 g) shredded low-moisture mozzarella cheese

MAKES ONE 12-INCH (30-CM) PIZZA; SERVES 2–4

Position an oven rack in the middle of the oven and place a pizza stone on the rack. Preheat the oven to 550°F/290°C (or as high as it will go). Once the oven has reached 550°F/290°C, let the stone continue to heat for 15–30 minutes longer, without opening the door.

Bring a small saucepan half full of salted water to a boil over high heat. Add the potato and cook, stirring occasionally, for about 10 minutes, or until just tender. Drain and set aside.

In a frying pan over medium heat, warm the olive oil. Add the garlic and cook, stirring occasionally, for about 2 minutes, or until soft but not browned. Add the spinach, season with salt and pepper, and cook, stirring often, for about 1 minute, or until the spinach mostly wilts. Transfer to a plate. Add the chorizo to the pan and cook, stirring occasionally and using your spoon to break up any clumps, for about 5 minutes, or until cooked through. Using a slotted spoon, transfer to paper towels to drain.

On a lightly floured surface, stretch the pizza dough into a 12-inch (30-cm) round. If the dough springs back, let it rest for about 10 minutes before continuing. Dust a pizza peel with semolina and transfer the dough round to the pizza peel.

Brush the edge of the dough round with olive oil. Leaving a 1-inch (2.5-cm) border, spread the sauce over the dough and top with the cheese. Distribute the spinach, then the chorizo, and then the potatoes over the pizza.

Carefully slide the pizza from the peel onto the hot stone in the oven and bake for about 8 minutes, or until the crust is golden brown. Using the peel, transfer the pizza to a cutting board. Let cool for about 1 minute, then slice and serve right away.

BROCCOLI RABE, SAUSAGE & SMOKED MOZZARELLA PIZZA

The mixture of sausage, slightly bitter broccoli rabe, garlic, and red pepper flakes is often reserved for pasta, but why not add it to a pizza? Sautéing the ingredients together with plenty of olive oil brings all the flavors together.

½ small bunch broccoli rabe, thick stems removed

2 tablespoons extra-virgin olive oil, plus more for brushing

½ lb (225 g) sweet or spicy Italian sausage, casings removed

6 cloves garlic, thinly sliced

¼ teaspoon red pepper flakes, or to taste

Kosher salt and freshly ground pepper

Semolina flour, for dusting

One 9-oz (250-g) ball NY Style Pizza Dough (page 98) or Whole Wheat Pizza Dough (page 96)

⅓–½ cup (80–120 ml) All-Purpose Pizza Sauce (page 106)

1 cup (115 g) shredded smoked mozzarella cheese

MAKES ONE 12-INCH (30-CM) PIZZA; SERVES 2–4

Position an oven rack in the middle of the oven and place a pizza stone on the rack. Preheat the oven to 550°F/290°C (or as high as it will go). Once the oven has reached 550°F/290°C, let the stone continue to heat for 15–30 minutes longer, without opening the door.

Bring a saucepan of water to a boil over high heat. Add the broccoli rabe and cook for about 3 minutes, or until the stems are tender-crisp. Drain well and let cool. When cool enough to handle, chop into ½-inch (12-mm) pieces. Set aside.

In a large frying pan over medium-high heat, warm the olive oil. Add the sausage and cook, stirring occasionally and using your spoon to break up any clumps, for about 5 minutes, or until no longer pink. Add the garlic and red pepper flakes and cook, stirring occasionally, for about 1 minute, or until the garlic just begins to soften but not brown. Add the broccoli rabe and stir to coat. Season to taste with salt and pepper. Remove from the heat and set aside.

On a lightly floured surface, stretch the pizza dough into a 12-inch (30-cm) round. If the dough springs back, let it rest for about 10 minutes before continuing. Dust a pizza peel with semolina and transfer the dough round to the pizza peel.

Brush the edge of the dough round with olive oil. Leaving a 1-inch (2.5-cm) border, spread the sauce over the dough and top with the cheese. Distribute the sausage–broccoli rabe mixture over the pizza.

Carefully slide the pizza from the peel onto the hot stone in the oven and bake for about 8 minutes, or until the crust is golden brown. Using the peel, transfer the pizza to a cutting board. Let cool for about 1 minute, then slice and serve right away.

MORTADELLA, PISTACHIO & BURRATA PIZZA

Most of the toppings on this unbelievably simple but delicious pizza are added after baking. A classic on many Italian menus, the mix of thinly sliced mortadella, crunchy–sweet pistachios, and extra–creamy burrata cheese makes this one pizza not to be missed.

Semolina flour, for dusting

One 9-oz (250-g) ball NY Style Pizza Dough (page 98)

Extra-virgin olive oil, for brushing

One 4-oz (115-g) ball fresh mozzarella cheese, sliced and chopped

6 thin slices mortadella

One 8-oz (225-g) ball burrata cheese

¼ cup (30 g) roasted and salted pistachios, roughly chopped

About 8 fresh basil leaves, roughly torn

MAKES ONE 12-INCH (30-CM) PIZZA; SERVES 2–4

Position an oven rack in the middle of the oven and place a pizza stone on the rack. Preheat the oven to 550°F/290°C (or as high as it will go). Once the oven has reached 550°F/290°C, let the stone continue to heat for 15–30 minutes longer, without opening the door.

On a lightly floured surface, stretch the pizza dough into a 12-inch (30-cm) round. If the dough springs back, let it rest for about 10 minutes before continuing. Dust a pizza peel with semolina and transfer the dough round to the pizza peel.

Brush the dough round with olive oil. Leaving a 1-inch (2.5-cm) border, sprinkle the mozzarella over the dough.

Carefully slide the pizza from the peel onto the hot stone in the oven and bake for about 8 minutes, or until the crust is golden brown. Using the peel, transfer the pizza to a cutting board. Let cool for about 1 minute, then cut the pizza into 6 slices. Arrange a folded slice of mortadella on each slice of pizza. Tear the burrata into bite-size pieces and distribute over the slices. Sprinkle with the pistachios and garnish with the basil. Serve right away.

FIG, PROSCIUTTO & GORGONZOLA PIZZA

Sweet fig jam and fresh juicy figs balance beautifully with thin slices of salty prosciutto and creamy Gorgonzola cheese in this exquisite pizza. A drizzle of aged balsamic is the perfect tangy addition. For a fresh note, add a tangle of baby arugula to the pizza before serving.

3 tablespoons unsalted butter

1 small yellow onion, thinly sliced

Kosher salt and freshly ground pepper

Semolina flour, for dusting

One 9-oz (250-g) ball NY Style Pizza Dough (page 98) or Whole Wheat Pizza Dough (page 96)

Extra-virgin olive oil, for brushing

3 tablespoons fig jam

2 oz (60 g) Gorgonzola cheese, crumbled

3 small figs, sliced or quartered

1 oz (30 g) thinly sliced prosciutto

Aged balsamic vinegar, for drizzling

MAKES ONE 12-INCH (30-CM) PIZZA; SERVES 2–4

Position an oven rack in the middle of the oven and place a pizza stone on the rack. Preheat the oven to 550°F/290°C (or as high as it will go). Once the oven has reached 550°F/290°C, let the stone continue to heat for 15–30 minutes longer, without opening the door.

Meanwhile, in a frying pan over low heat, melt the butter. Add the onion and season with salt and pepper. Cook, stirring occasionally, for about 40 minutes, or until the onion is meltingly tender and rich brown in color; do not let it burn. Let cool.

On a lightly floured surface, stretch the pizza dough into a 12-inch (30-cm) round or oval. If the dough springs back, let it rest for about 10 minutes before continuing. Dust a pizza peel with semolina and transfer the dough round to the pizza peel.

Brush the edge of the dough round with olive oil. Leaving a 1-inch (2.5-cm) border, spread the fig jam over the dough. Sprinkle with the Gorgonzola and top with the caramelized onion.

Carefully slide the pizza from the peel onto the hot stone in the oven and bake for about 5 minutes, or until the crust is firm but not crisp. Using the peel, remove the pizza from the oven and top with the fig slices. Bake for 2–3 minutes longer, or until the figs are slightly caramelized and the crust is crisp and golden brown. Using the peel, transfer the pizza to a cutting board. Drape the prosciutto over the pizza and drizzle with vinegar. Let cool for about 1 minute, then slice and serve right away.

CHICKEN CAESAR PIADINE

Crisp-cooked thin pizza crust is a terrific base for any of the salads in this book.
Here, the Caesar salad also makes a great side dish for your favorite pizza.
If you like, substitute grilled shrimp or thinly sliced flank steak for the chicken.

2 boneless, skin-on chicken breast halves (500 g total)

⅓ cup (80 ml) plus 1 tablespoon extra-virgin olive oil, plus more for brushing

Kosher salt and freshly ground pepper

1 clove garlic, chopped

2 anchovy fillets

1 tablespoon fresh lemon juice

1 large egg yolk

1 teaspoon Worcestershire sauce

6 tablespoons (45 g) grated Parmesan cheese

Two 9-oz (250-g) balls NY Style Pizza Dough (page 98)

Semolina flour, for dusting

2 teaspoons fresh thyme leaves, chopped

2 hearts of romaine lettuce, cored and chopped

MAKES FOUR 8-INCH (20-CM) PIADINE; SERVES 4

Position 2 oven racks in the middle and in the lower third of the oven. Place a pizza stone on the lower rack. Preheat the oven to 375°F/190°C.

Pat the chicken dry and put it on a small baking sheet. Brush with 1 tablespoon of the olive oil and season with salt and pepper. Roast the chicken on the middle rack for 20–25 minutes, or until opaque throughout. Remove from the oven and let cool. When cool enough to handle, discard the skin and chop or shred the chicken into bite-size pieces. Set aside. Move the pizza stone to the middle rack and raise the oven temperature to 550°F/290°C (or as high as it will go).

To make the dressing, in a blender, combine the garlic, anchovies, lemon juice, egg yolk, and Worcestershire sauce and process until smooth. With the motor running, add the remaining ⅓ cup (80 ml) olive oil in a steady stream and blend until well combined. Stop the machine, add 3 tablespoons of the Parmesan, and pulse to mix. Taste and adjust the seasoning with salt and pepper. Set aside.

To make the piadine, divide the pizza dough into 4 equal pieces. On a lightly floured surface, stretch each piece into an 8-inch (20-cm) round. If the dough springs back, let it rest for about 10 minutes before continuing. Brush each dough round with olive oil, sprinkle with the thyme, and season with salt and pepper.

Dust a pizza peel with semolina and transfer a dough round to the pizza peel. Carefully slide the piadine from the peel onto the hot stone in the oven and bake for 4–6 minutes, or until golden brown. Using the peel, remove from the oven, then transfer to a plate. Repeat with the remaining piadine, transferring each to a separate plate.

While the piadine are baking, assemble the salad. In a large bowl, toss the lettuce with the dressing, the remaining Parmesan, and the chicken. Top each piadine with the chicken salad and serve right away.

BUTTERNUT SQUASH, BACON & CARAMELIZED ONION PIZZA WITH ARUGULA

Sweet, dense butternut squash paired with smoky bacon and rich caramelized onions is a delicious trinity. Salty crumbles of feta and peppery arugula add just right balance to finish this elegant pizza. For a full meal, serve with a full-bodied white wine and a Grilled Romaine Salad with Anchovy-Mustard Vinaigrette (page 83).

3 cups (425 g) peeled and cubed butternut squash, cut into ½-inch (12-mm) pieces

3 tablespoons extra-virgin olive oil, plus more for brushing and drizzling

1 teaspoon minced fresh thyme

Kosher salt and freshly ground pepper

1 large yellow onion, halved and thinly sliced

6 slices thick-cut applewood-smoked bacon, chopped

Semolina flour, for dusting

Two 9-oz (250-g) balls Whole Wheat Pizza Dough (page 96) or NY Style Pizza Dough (page 98)

4 oz (115 g) feta or goat cheese, crumbled

¼ cup (30 g) grated Parmesan cheese

½ cup (15 g) baby arugula

MAKES TWO 12-INCH (30-CM) PIZZAS; SERVES 4–6

Position 2 oven racks in the middle and in the lower third of the oven and preheat to 450°F/230°C. Place a pizza stone on the lower rack.

Pile the squash on a large rimmed baking sheet, add 2 tablespoons of the olive oil and the thyme, and season with salt and pepper. Toss to coat well, then spread in an even layer. Bake, stirring once or twice, until fork-tender, about 15 minutes.

Meanwhile, in a large frying pan over low heat, warm the remaining 1 tablespoon olive oil. Add the onion and cook, stirring occasionally, for about 20 minutes, or until tender and golden. Transfer to a bowl. In the same pan, fry the bacon over medium heat, stirring, for about 6 minutes, or until crisp.

Move the pizza stone to the middle rack and raise the oven temperature to 550°F/290°C (or as high as it will go).

On a lightly floured surface, stretch 1 ball of pizza dough into a 12-inch (30-cm) round. If the dough springs back, let it rest for about 10 minutes before continuing. Dust a pizza peel with semolina and transfer the dough round to the pizza peel.

Brush the edge of the dough round with olive oil. Leaving a ½-inch (12-mm) border, spread half of the caramelized onions over the dough, then top with half each of the butternut squash and bacon. Sprinkle with half each of the feta and Parmesan.

Carefully slide the pizza from the peel onto the hot stone in the oven and bake for about 8 minutes, or until the crust is golden brown. Using the peel, transfer the pizza to a cutting board. Drizzle with olive oil. Let cool for about 1 minute, then top with half of the arugula, slice, and serve right away. Repeat with the second dough ball.

GRILLED PIZZA WITH PROSCIUTTO, MOZZARELLA & HOT HONEY

Hot honey is wonderfully versatile, and there's no better way to experience it than drizzled over a smoke-kissed pizza piled high with salty prosciutto. If you like, add thin slices of grilled peaches to the pie before cooking, then sprinkle baby arugula over the top just before serving.

¼ cup (90 g) honey

2 teaspoons
hot pepper sauce

¼ teaspoon
red pepper flakes,
or to taste

Extra-virgin olive oil,
for brushing

Semolina flour, for dusting

Two 9-oz (250-g) balls
NY Style Pizza Dough
(page 98)

⅔ cup (160 ml) All-Purpose
Pizza Sauce (page 106)

¾ lb (340 g) fresh mozzarella
cheese, thinly sliced

2 oz (60 g) thinly sliced
prosciutto

**MAKES TWO 10-INCH
(25-CM) PIZZAS;
SERVES 4–6**

Prepare a gas or charcoal grill for direct and indirect grilling over medium heat (350°–450°F/180°–230°C). Brush the grill grate clean.

In a small bowl, stir together the honey, hot pepper sauce, and red pepper flakes. Set aside.

Brush two 12-inch (30-cm) squares of aluminum foil on one side with olive oil; place each on a baking sheet. On a lightly floured surface, stretch 1 dough ball into a flat disk. Place in the center of 1 of the foil sheets and stretch the dough into a 10-inch (25-cm) round. Brush the top of the dough all over with olive oil. Repeat with the other dough ball.

Invert 1 dough round directly onto the hotter side of the grill. Using tongs, carefully peel the foil off the dough. Grill with the lid closed for 1–3 minutes, or until the dough is nicely browned on the bottom and almost dry on top. About halfway through (when the dough is cooked enough to move easily), use the tongs to rotate the dough 90 degrees to prevent burning.

Using a pizza peel, transfer the grilled dough round to a cutting board, grilled side up. Repeat with the second dough round.

Brush the grilled tops of both pizzas with olive oil. Top each with half of the sauce, then half of the mozzarella and prosciutto. One at a time, place a pizza back on the grill. Cover the grill and cook, rotating each round about 90 degrees halfway through, until the bottoms brown and the cheese melts, 1–3 minutes. Slide the pizza to the cooler side of the grill to finish melting the cheese, 2–3 minutes longer.

Using the pizza peel, transfer the pizza to the cutting board. Repeat with the second pizza. To serve, drizzle some of the hot pepper honey over the pizzas. Slice and serve right away.

MUSHROOM, PEPPERONI & BLACK OLIVE SHEET PAN PIZZA

Thick, fluffy sheet pan pizza is not only easy to prepare, but also can be made mostly in advance. And it's also a kid favorite, so top it with whatever ingredients you like, although pepperoni, mushrooms, and sliced black olives are a pizza parlor classic.

Sheet Pan Pizza Dough (page 102), partially baked

2 tablespoons extra-virgin olive oil, plus more for brushing

8 oz (225 g) cremini or button mushrooms, brushed clean and thickly sliced

1 teaspoon dried oregano

Kosher salt and freshly ground pepper

¾ cup (180 ml) All-Purpose Pizza Sauce (page 106) or Spicy Arrabiata Sauce (page 111)

1½ cups (170 g) shredded low-moisture mozzarella cheese

3 oz (90 g) pepperoni slices

⅓ cup (45 g) pitted black olives, such as Kalamata, halved lengthwise

MAKES 1 LARGE SHEET PAN PIZZA; SERVES 6

Partially bake the sheet pan pizza dough as directed in the recipe. If the dough was frozen, let thaw completely and come to room temperature.

Position an oven rack in the upper third of the oven and preheat to 450°F/230°C.

In a frying pan over medium-high heat, warm the olive oil. Add the mushrooms and oregano and season with salt and pepper. Cook, stirring occasionally, for about 5 minutes, or until the mushrooms are softened and slightly browned around the edges. Remove from the heat and set aside.

Brush the dough lightly with olive oil. Leaving a ½-inch (12-mm) border, spread the sauce over the dough and top with the cheese. Distribute the pepperoni, mushrooms, and olives over the pizza.

Bake the pizza on the upper rack for 18 minutes, or until the crust is golden brown. Slide the pizza off the baking sheet and onto a cutting board. Let cool for a few minutes, then slice and serve right away.

SAUSAGE, PEPERONCINI & MOZZARELLA CALZONE

Making a large calzone is slightly easier—and faster—than creating individual calzones, but if you like, divide the dough into 4 smaller ones. Don't leave out the pepperoncini, as they give the calzone a spicy, vinegary kick that nicely balances the richness of the sausage.

½ lb (225 g) sweet Italian sausage, casings removed

Semolina flour, for dusting

One 9-oz (250-g) ball NY Style Pizza Dough (page 98)

1 large egg, beaten with 1 teaspoon water, for egg wash

⅓–½ cup (80–120 ml) All-Purpose Pizza Sauce (page 106)

1 cup (115 g) shredded low-moisture mozzarella cheese

2 tablespoons grated Parmesan cheese

¼ cup (40 g) pickled peperoncini, or to taste, drained and sliced

4–6 fresh basil leaves, torn into large pieces

Kosher salt and freshly ground pepper

MAKES 1 LARGE CALZONE; SERVES 2

Position an oven rack in the middle of the oven and place a pizza stone on the rack. Preheat the oven to 550°F/290°C (or as high as it will go). Once the oven has reached 550°F/290°C, let the stone continue to heat for 15–30 minutes longer, without opening the door.

In a frying pan over medium-high heat, cook, stirring occasionally and using your spoon to break up any clumps, for about 5 minutes, or until cooked through. Using a slotted spoon, transfer to paper towels to drain.

On a lightly floured surface, stretch the pizza dough into a 12-inch (30-cm) round. If the dough springs back, let it rest for about 10 minutes before continuing. Dust a pizza peel with semolina and transfer the dough round to the pizza peel.

Brush half of the dough round with some of the egg wash. Leaving a 1-inch (2.5-cm) border, spread half of the sauce over one-half of the dough round. Top with the sausage, mozzarella, Parmesan, peperoncini, and basil, then top with the remaining sauce. Season lightly with salt and pepper.

Fold the uncovered half of the calzone up and over the filling to meet the opposite edges, then crimp the edges of the dough tightly to seal. Brush the top of the calzone with egg wash. Using the tip of a sharp knife, make a slit in the top of the calzone.

Carefully slide the calzone from the peel onto the hot stone in the oven. Bake for about 8 minutes, or until the crust is golden brown. Using the peel, transfer the calzone to a cutting board or wire rack and let cool for 5 minutes, then serve right away.

DEEP DISH DOUBLE MEAT PIZZA

This pizza is for all you meat lovers out there. Baked in a cast-iron pan, the crunchy-tender cornmeal crust envelops both sausage and pepperoni, plus sautéed mushrooms, red bell peppers, and olives, with plenty of sauce and cheese. It's sure to satiate even the heartiest appetite.

¾ lb (340 g) sweet or hot Italian sausage, casings removed

1 tablespoon extra-virgin olive oil, plus more for brushing

1 small red bell pepper, seeded and chopped

5 oz (140 g) cremini or button mushrooms, brushed clean and sliced

Kosher salt and freshly ground pepper

One ball Deep Dish Cornmeal Pizza Dough (page 103)

1½ oz (40 g) sliced pepperoni

¼ cup (35 g) pitted and sliced black olives (optional)

1 cup (240 ml) All-Purpose Pizza Sauce (page 106)

1¼ cups (140 g) shredded low-moisture mozzarella cheese

¼ cup (30 g) grated Parmesan cheese

MAKES ONE 10-INCH (25-CM) DEEP DISH PIZZA; SERVES 4–6

Position a rack in the lower third of the oven and preheat to 400°F/200°C.

In a large frying pan over medium-high heat, cook the sausage, stirring occasionally and using your spoon to break up any clumps, for about 5 minutes, or until cooked through. Using a slotted spoon, transfer to paper towels to drain.

Pour off the fat in the pan and return the pan to medium-high heat. Add the olive oil, bell pepper, and mushrooms, season with salt and pepper, and cook, stirring occasionally, for 4–5 minutes, or until the vegetables are softened and browned around the edges. Remove from the heat and set aside.

Brush a 10-inch (25-cm) cast-iron frying pan generously with olive oil. Put the pizza dough in the pan and pat into a disk. Using your hands, press the dough into the pan, nudging it gently into an even layer on the bottom and halfway up the sides. Brush the dough with more olive oil and top with the sausage, pepper and mushroom mixture, pepperoni, and olives (if using). Pour the sauce over, spread it evenly, and sprinkle with the mozzarella and then the Parmesan.

Bake for about 35 minutes, or until the bottom of the dough is nicely browned (lift carefully with a spatula or long-bladed knife to peek). Remove from the oven and let cool for 5 minutes. Slice the pizza directly in the pan and serve right away.

GRILLED BARBECUED CHICKEN PIZZA WITH SMOKED CHEDDAR

With layers of barbecue sauce, grilled chicken, smoked Cheddar, and sweet corn kernels, this isn't your standard pizza. But the superb combination of flavors evokes a summertime barbecue, best washed down with an ice-cold beer.

Extra-virgin olive oil, for brushing

Semolina flour, for dusting

Two 9-oz (250-g) balls NY Style Pizza Dough (page 98)

⅔ cup (160 ml) homemade Barbecue Sauce (page 115) or store-bought

About 1½ cups (250 g) chopped grilled chicken

1½ cups (170 g) shredded smoked Cheddar cheese

½ small red onion, sliced paper-thin

½ cup (85 g) fresh or grilled corn kernels

¼ cup (40 g) chopped jarred roasted red bell peppers, drained

¼ cup (15 g) chopped fresh cilantro

Kosher salt

MAKES TWO 10-INCH (25-CM) PIZZAS; SERVES 4–6

Prepare a gas or charcoal grill for direct and indirect grilling over medium heat (350°–450°F/180°–230°C). Brush the grill grate clean.

Brush two 12-inch (30-cm) squares of aluminum foil on one side with olive oil; place each on a baking sheet. On a lightly floured surface, stretch 1 dough ball into a flat disk. Place in the center of 1 of the foil sheets and stretch the dough into a 10-inch (25-cm) round. Brush the top of the dough all over with olive oil. Repeat with the other dough ball.

Invert 1 dough round directly onto the hotter side of the grill. Using tongs, carefully peel the foil off the dough. Grill with the lid closed for 1–3 minutes, or until the dough is nicely browned on the bottom and almost dry on top. About halfway through (when the dough is cooked enough to move easily), use the tongs to rotate the dough 90 degrees to prevent burning.

Using a pizza peel, transfer the grilled dough round to a cutting board, grilled side up. Repeat with the second dough round.

Spread half of the barbecue sauce over the grilled side of each pizza. Top each with half of the chicken, cheese, onion, corn, and roasted peppers.

One at a time, place a pizza back on the grill on the hotter side of the grill. Cover the grill and cook, rotating each round about 90 degrees halfway through the cooking, until the bottoms brown and the cheese melts, 1–3 minutes. Slide the pizza to the cooler side of the grill, cover the grill, and cook for 2–3 minutes longer, or until the cheese finishes melting.

Using the pizza peel, transfer the pizza to the cutting board. Repeat with the second pizza. To serve, top each pizza with half of the cilantro and season with salt. Slice and serve right away.

FRESH CLAM PIZZA WITH CREAMY GARLIC SAUCE

Fresh clams will undoubtedly produce the best results for this pizza, but in a pinch, you can use canned or frozen ones. Look for whole-belly clams, rather than prechopped clams, which can turn chewy when cooked.

2 tablespoons extra-virgin olive oil, plus more for brushing

1 shallot, finely chopped

2 cloves garlic, thinly sliced

1 lb (450 g) littleneck clams, soaked in salted water for 30 minutes, then drained

¼ cup (60 ml) dry white wine

1 tablespoon unsalted butter

Kosher salt and freshly ground pepper

Semolina flour, for dusting

One 9-oz (250-g) ball NY Style Pizza Dough (page 98)

⅓ cup (80 ml) Creamy Garlic Sauce (page 114)

2 tablespoons chopped fresh flat-leaf parsley

Lemon wedges, for serving

MAKES ONE 12-INCH (30-CM) PIZZA; SERVES 2–4

In a large saucepan over medium heat, warm the oil. Add the shallot and cook, stirring occasionally, until softened, about 3 minutes. Add the garlic and cook, stirring, for 1 minute. Add the clams and stir to coat.

Add the wine and butter and stir until the butter melts, about 2 minutes. Reduce the heat to low, cover, and cook until the clams have opened, 10–12 minutes. Using a slotted spoon, transfer the clams to a bowl. Discard any clams that did not open. Cook the wine sauce over medium-low heat, stirring often, until reduced by half, about 15 minutes. Season with salt and pepper.

Position an oven rack in the middle of the oven and place a pizza stone on the rack. Preheat the oven to 550°F/290°C (or as high as it will go). Once the oven has reached 550°F/290°C, let the stone continue to heat for 15–30 minutes longer, without opening the door.

Meanwhile, remove about two-thirds of the clams from their shells and coarsely chop the meat; reserve the remaining clams for topping the pizza. Stir the clam meat into the wine sauce and set aside.

On a lightly floured surface, stretch the pizza dough into a 12-inch (30-cm) round. If the dough springs back, let it rest for about 10 minutes before continuing. Dust a pizza peel with semolina and transfer the dough round to the pizza peel.

Brush the edge of the dough round with olive oil. Leaving a 1-inch (2.5-cm) border, spread the creamy garlic sauce evenly over the dough. Spread the clam–wine sauce evenly over the creamy garlic sauce.

Slide the pizza from the peel onto the hot stone. Bake until the crust is golden, about 6 minutes. Using the pizza peel, remove the pizza from the oven and top with the clams. Bake until the clams are just heated through, about 3 minutes longer. Using the pizza peel, transfer the pizza to a cutting board. Garnish with the parsley. Slice and serve right away.

SHRIMP & FETA PIZZA WITH ROASTED RED PEPPER PESTO

Halving the shrimp lengthwise makes it easier to nestle them (cut side down) into the toppings so they cook evenly. The addition of feta, red pepper, and fresh oregano gives this pizza a decidedly Greek flavor.

Semolina flour, for dusting

One 9-oz (250-g) ball NY Style Pizza Dough (page 98) or Whole Wheat Pizza Dough (page 96)

1 tablespoon extra-virgin olive oil, plus more for brushing

½ cup (120 ml) Roasted Red Pepper Pesto (page 110)

⅓ cup (45 g) crumbled feta cheese

1 tablespoon fresh oregano leaves

½ lb (225 g) medium shrimp, peeled, deveined, and halved lengthwise

Kosher salt and freshly ground pepper

MAKES ONE 12-INCH (30-CM) PIZZA; SERVES 2–4

Position an oven rack in the middle of the oven and place a pizza stone on the rack. Preheat the oven to 550°F/290°C (or as high as it will go). Once the oven has reached 550°F/290°C, let the stone continue to heat for 15–30 minutes longer, without opening the door.

On a lightly floured surface, stretch the pizza dough into a 12-inch (30-cm) round. If the dough springs back, let it rest for about 10 minutes before continuing. Dust a pizza peel with semolina and transfer the dough round to the pizza peel.

Brush the edge of the dough round with olive oil. Leaving a 1-inch (2.5-cm) border, spread the pesto over the dough and top with the feta and half of the oregano.

In a bowl, toss the shrimp with the olive oil and season with salt and pepper. Chop the remaining oregano and toss with the shrimp. Arrange the shrimp, cut side down, on top of the pizza.

Carefully slide the pizza from the peel onto the hot stone in the oven and bake for about 8 minutes, or until the crust is golden brown. Using the peel, transfer the pizza to a cutting board. Let cool for about 1 minute, then slice and serve right away.

SPICY MARINARA PIZZA WITH ANCHOVIES, OLIVES & CAPERS

All of the ingredients of a classic puttanesca sauce come together in this rich, savory pizza—which also happens to be dairy free. Use a light hand when seasoning this pie, as many of the toppings are naturally salty.

Semolina flour, for dusting

One 9-oz (250-g) ball NY Style Pizza Dough (page 98) or Whole Wheat Pizza Dough (page 96)

Extra-virgin olive oil, for brushing and drizzling

½ cup (120 ml) Spicy Arrabiata Sauce (page 111)

¼ cup (35 g) Kalamata olives, pitted and halved lengthwise

2 tablespoons brined capers, drained

6 anchovy fillets

1–2 teaspoons chopped fresh oregano

MAKES ONE 12-INCH (30-CM) PIZZA; SERVES 2–4

Position an oven rack in the middle of the oven and place a pizza stone on the rack. Preheat the oven to 550°F/290°C (or as high as it will go). Once the oven has reached 550°F/290°C, let the stone continue to heat for 15–30 minutes longer, without opening the door.

On a lightly floured surface, stretch the pizza dough into a 12-inch (30-cm) round. If the dough springs back, let it rest for about 10 minutes before continuing. Dust a pizza peel with semolina and transfer the dough round to the pizza peel.

Brush the edge of the dough round with olive oil. Leaving a 1-inch (2.5-cm) border, spread the sauce over the dough. Distribute the olives, capers, and anchovies evenly over the pizza, then sprinkle with the oregano. Drizzle with a olive oil.

Carefully slide the pizza from the peel onto the hot stone in the oven and bake for about 8 minutes, or until the crust is golden brown. Using the peel, transfer the pizza to a cutting board. Let cool for about 1 minute, then slice and serve.

SMOKED SALMON, CRÈME FRAÎCHE & DILL PIZZETTES

These elegant and versatile pizzettes would be perfect for a springtime brunch or as part of a larger spread for an evening gathering. Baking the red onions on the dough mellows and sweetens them.

1 cup (225 g) crème fraîche or sour cream

Grated zest of 1 lemon

1 tablespoon fresh lemon juice

2 tablespoons chopped fresh dill, plus small sprigs for garnish

2 tablespoons chopped fresh chives

Kosher salt and freshly ground pepper

½ small red onion, thinly sliced

1 teaspoon extra-virgin olive oil, plus more for brushing

Two 9-oz (250-g) balls NY Style Pizza Dough (page 98)

Semolina flour, for dusting

8 oz (225 g) thinly sliced smoked salmon, chopped or torn into small pieces

MAKES EIGHT 6-INCH (15-CM) PIZZETTES; SERVES 6–8

Position an oven rack in the middle of the oven and place a pizza stone on the rack. Preheat the oven to 550°F/290°C (or as high as it will go). Once the oven has reached 550°F/290°C, let the stone continue to heat for 15–30 minutes longer, without opening the door.

In a small bowl, stir together the crème fraîche, lemon zest and juice, dill, and chives. Season to taste with salt and pepper. Set aside at room temperature. In another small bowl, toss the onion with the olive oil and season lightly with salt and pepper. Set aside.

Divide the pizza dough into 8 equal pieces.

On a lightly floured surface, stretch each piece into a 6-inch (15-cm) round. If the dough springs back, let it rest for about 10 minutes before continuing. Dust a pizza peel with semolina and transfer 2 dough rounds to the pizza peel.

Working with 2 dough rounds at a time, brush each dough round with olive oil. Top with some of the onion slices.

Carefully slide the pizzettes from the peel onto the hot stone in the oven and bake for 4–5 minutes, or until the crust is golden brown. Using the peel, transfer the pizzettes to a cutting board. Let cool for a few minutes, then dollop 2 tablespoons of the crème fraîche mixture on each. Scatter 1 oz (30 g) of the smoked salmon on top of each pizzette. Garnish with a dill sprig and serve right away.

Repeat to cook the remaining pizzettes. With practice, you can fit 4 of the pizzettes at a time on the stone.

SIDES

HEIRLOOM TOMATO SALAD WITH BURRATA & PESTO

Choose juicy ripe tomatoes at the peak of their summer ripeness for the very best version of this salad. A combination of different-colored tomatoes and types, including heirlooms, grape, and cherry tomatoes, add to a stunning presentation. You can also swap regular fresh mozzarella for the creamier burrata.

3 tablespoons Classic Basil Pesto (page 109)

1½ tablespoons red wine vinegar

¼ cup (60 ml) extra-virgin olive oil

Kosher salt and freshly ground pepper

3 large tomatoes, preferably heirlooms, sliced

About 3 cups (510 g) mixed red, yellow, and orange cherry tomatoes, halved

1 large ball burrata or fresh mozzarella cheese

Small fresh basil leaves, for garnish

MAKES 4–6 SERVINGS

In a small bowl, whisk together the pesto and vinegar. Add the olive oil in a thin stream, whisking constantly until the dressing is well blended. Season to taste with salt and pepper.

Arrange the tomatoes decoratively on a platter. Season the tomatoes with salt and pepper. Nestle the burrata in the center. Drizzle the burrata and tomatoes with the pesto dressing. Garnish with basil leaves and serve right away.

GRILLED ROMAINE SALAD WITH ANCHOVY-MUSTARD VINAIGRETTE

This updated variation on Caesar salad is ideal to make alongside any of the grilled pizzas in this book—or if you are also preparing the Grilled Vegetables with Balsamic & Thyme (page 93). A grilled salad might seem odd, but the grill imparts incredible flavor to the hearty romaine, and the lettuce stands up well to the assertive vinaigrette.

ANCHOVY-MUSTARD
VINAIGRETTE

1 clove garlic, minced

6 anchovy fillets, minced

1 tablespoon country Dijon mustard

1 large egg yolk

½ cup (120 ml) extra-virgin olive oil

Juice of 1 lemon

Kosher salt and freshly ground pepper

2 heads romaine lettuce, quartered lengthwise

2 tablespoons extra-virgin olive oil

¼ cup (30 g) grated Parmesan cheese

MAKES 4 SERVINGS

Prepare a gas or charcoal grill for direct and indirect grilling over medium heat (350°–450°F/180°–230°C). Brush the grill grate clean.

To make the vinaigrette, in a bowl, combine the garlic and anchovy fillets and mash with the back of a fork until a paste forms. Whisk in the mustard and egg yolk, then whisk in the olive oil, a little at a time, until a thick sauce forms. Stir in the lemon juice and season to taste with salt and pepper. Set aside.

Coat the romaine quarters with the olive oil. Put them on the grate directly over the heat and grill, turning once, until just grill-marked, about 20 seconds per side. Using tongs, move the romaine away from the heat. Coat the romaine with half of the vinaigrette, drizzling it down into the leaves, then sprinkle with half of the cheese. Cover the grill and cook until the cheese just starts to melt and the ends of the lettuce wedges wilt, about 2 minutes.

Transfer the romaine to a platter. Dress with the remaining vinaigrette and a scattering of the remaining cheese. Serve right away.

ANTIPASTI SALAD WITH PEPERONCINI VINAIGRETTE

This fresh twist on the classic pizza parlor staple features sweet cherry tomatoes, avocados, provolone cheese, and prosciutto, all drizzled with a piquant peperoncini vinaigrette. If you like, add chopped salami, halved fresh ovoline mozzarella, butter beans, or chopped roasted red bell peppers.

PEPERONCINI VINAIGRETTE

¼ cup (60 ml) red wine vinegar

5 peperoncini, stemmed, seeded, and minced

1 tablespoon minced fresh oregano

2 teaspoons sugar

¼ teaspoon kosher salt

6 tablespoons (90 ml) extra-virgin olive oil

4 cups (680 g) cherry or grape tomatoes, halved

¼ teaspoon kosher salt, plus more as needed

3 avocados

8 oz (225 g) provolone cheese, cut into ½-inch (12-mm) cubes

1–2 cups (35–70 g) arugula leaves

10 oz (285 g) thinly sliced prosciutto

MAKES 6 SERVINGS

To make the vinaigrette, in a small bowl, whisk together the vinegar, peperoncini, oregano, sugar, and salt. Add the olive oil in a thin stream, whisking until the vinaigrette is well blended. Set aside.

In a medium bowl, toss the tomatoes with the salt and let stand until they release their juices, about 5 minutes, then drain. Pit and peel the avocados and cut them crosswise into slices about ½ inch (12 mm) thick. Sprinkle with a large pinch of salt.

Arrange the tomatoes, avocados, cheese, and arugula on a large platter. Whisk the vinaigrette to recombine, then drizzle it over the arranged salad. Arrange the prosciutto on the platter and serve right away.

CHOPPED SALAD WITH TARRAGON BUTTERMILK DRESSING

Chopped salad can include nearly any combination of crunchy vegetables, greens, nuts, and other ingredients that are cut into small, uniform pieces and tossed in a big bowl with dressing. It's a great formula for using up leftovers. To make a heartier version, add chunks of cheese, chopped salami, or shredded rotisserie chicken.

2 tablespoons minced garlic

2 tablespoons minced shallot

5 tablespoons (80 g) sour cream

¼ cup (60 ml) buttermilk

2 tablespoons fresh lemon juice

2 teaspoons chopped fresh tarragon

½ teaspoon kosher salt, plus more as needed

¼ teaspoon freshly ground pepper, plus more as needed

1 heart of romaine lettuce, cored and chopped

1 small head radicchio, cored and chopped

½ English cucumber, chopped

8 small radishes, chopped

1½ cups (250 g) cherry tomatoes, halved or quartered

1 cup (140 g) hazelnuts, toasted and chopped

MAKES 6 SERVINGS

To make the dressing, in a small bowl, whisk together the garlic, shallot, sour cream, buttermilk, lemon juice, tarragon, salt, and pepper until well blended. Set aside.

In a large salad bowl, combine the lettuce, radicchio, cucumber, radishes, tomatoes, and hazelnuts and toss to mix. Pour in the dressing and toss to coat all the ingredients well. Taste and adjust the seasoning with salt and pepper. Serve right away.

WARM SPINACH & BACON SALAD

This spinach salad is not only delicious but also full of nutrients, and is a great sidekick to any pizza. Marinated mushrooms bring zing along with a mustard-infused balsamic dressing. Bacon, hard-boiled eggs, and cherry tomatoes add heartiness and flavor.

8 tablespoons (120 ml) extra-virgin olive oil

1 lb (450 g) button mushrooms, brushed clean and halved

1½ tablespoons fresh lemon juice

2 cloves garlic, thinly sliced

1 teaspoon minced fresh thyme

¼ teaspoon red pepper flakes

Kosher salt and freshly ground pepper

3 large eggs

10 oz (285 g) baby spinach

6 slices thick-cut applewood-smoked bacon, chopped

3 tablespoons balsamic vinegar

1 tablespoon whole-grain mustard

1 small red onion, thinly sliced

1½ cups (250 g) cherry tomatoes, halved

MAKES 6–8 SERVINGS

In a frying pan over medium-high heat, warm 2 tablespoons of the olive oil. Add the mushrooms and cook, stirring occasionally, until they release their juices and brown lightly, 5–6 minutes. Transfer to a medium bowl. Add 4 tablespoons (60 ml) of the olive oil, the lemon juice, garlic, thyme, red pepper flakes and salt and pepper to taste and toss to coat. Let marinate for at least 1 hour.

To hard-boil the eggs, place them in a saucepan just large enough to hold them. Add cold water to cover by 1 inch (2.5 cm) and bring just to a boil over high heat. Remove the pan from the heat, cover, and let stand for 15 minutes. Have ready a bowl of ice water. Drain the eggs, then transfer to the ice water and let cool. Peel and coarsely chop the eggs.

Put the spinach in a large bowl. In a frying pan over medium heat, fry the bacon, stirring, until crisp, about 6 minutes. Transfer to paper towels to drain. Pour off all but 2 tablespoons of the fat in the pan. Off the heat, whisk the vinegar and mustard into the fat in the pan, then whisk in the remaining 2 tablespoons olive oil. Season with salt and pepper, drizzle over the spinach, and toss to coat well.

Divide the spinach among individual plates and top with the onion, tomatoes, marinated mushrooms, chopped eggs, and bacon. Serve right away.

ASPARAGUS-ARUGULA SALAD WITH LEMON & PARMESAN

This simplest of salads is ideal when pencil-thin asparagus hits the farmers' markets. But if you've already fired up the grill, use thicker spears and grill just until crisp-tender. Let them cool, then chop and add to the salad.

3½ lb (1.6 kg) pencil-thin asparagus

3 cups (105 g) baby arugula

1 large lemon

¼ teaspoon kosher salt, plus more as needed

¼ teaspoon freshly ground pepper, plus more as needed

2 tablespoons extra-virgin olive oil

Parmesan cheese, for shaving

MAKES 6 SERVINGS

Bring a large saucepan two-thirds full of salted water to a boil over high heat. Have ready a bowl of ice water. Trim off the tough end of each asparagus spear and cut the spears on the diagonal into 1½-inch (4-cm) lengths.

Add the asparagus pieces to the boiling water and cook until the asparagus is crisp-tender and bright green, about 1 minute. Drain and then immediately plunge the asparagus into the ice water. Let stand until cool, about 2 minutes, then drain again and pat dry. Transfer to a serving platter and toss with the arugula.

Finely grate 1 tablespoon zest from the lemon, then halve and squeeze 1 tablespoon juice. In a small bowl, whisk together the lemon zest and juice, salt, and pepper. Add the olive oil in a thin stream, whisking constantly until the vinaigrette is well blended. Taste and adjust the seasoning with salt and pepper.

Drizzle the vinaigrette evenly over the salad and toss to coat. Using a vegetable peeler, shave the cheese over the top and serve right away.

SHAVED ZUCCHINI WITH FETA, LEMON & MINT

Summer's bounty of zucchini and summer squash is the centerpiece of this super-fresh salad. A wide vegetable peeler is the best bet for cutting the zucchini lengthwise into thin ribbons. For a pretty presentation, use half zucchini and half yellow squash.

4 zucchini (about 1 kg total)

¼ cup (60 ml) extra-virgin olive oil

1 teaspoon grated lemon zest

¼ teaspoon kosher salt, plus more as needed

¼ teaspoon freshly ground pepper, plus more as needed

¼ cup (15 g) torn fresh mint leaves

5 oz (140 g) feta cheese, crumbled

MAKES 4–6 SERVINGS

Trim the zucchini but do not peel it. Using a sharp vegetable peeler, shave the zucchini lengthwise into long, thin strips, letting the strips fall into a bowl.

In a small bowl, whisk together the olive oil and lemon zest. Drizzle this mixture over the zucchini and season with the salt and pepper. Add the mint and cheese to the bowl and toss gently. Taste and adjust the seasoning with salt and pepper and serve right away.

GRILLED VEGETABLES
WITH BALSAMIC & THYME

A platter brimming with the best of summer vegetables makes a terrific side dish to nearly every pizza in this book. It's easy to vary the ingredients based on what's in season—swap in sugar snap peas or leeks in spring and sweet potatoes or broccolini in the fall. If it's too cold to grill, simply brush the vinaigrette on the vegetables and roast in the oven instead.

6 tablespoons (90 ml) extra-virgin olive oil

¼ cup (60 ml) balsamic vinegar

1 red onion, cut into wedges

1 Italian eggplant, cut into ½-inch (12-mm) slices

2 red and/or yellow bell peppers, seeded and quartered

3 squashes, such as zucchini or pattypan, cut on the diagonal into slices about ½ inch (12 mm) thick

1 bunch thick asparagus, trimmed

¼ cup (10 g) fresh thyme leaves, chopped

Kosher salt and freshly ground pepper

MAKES 4–6 SERVINGS

Prepare a gas or charcoal grill for direct grilling over medium-high heat (450°F/230°C). Brush the grill grate clean.

In a small bowl, whisk together the olive oil and vinegar. Arrange the onion, eggplant, bell peppers, squashes, and asparagus on a baking sheet. Brush on all sides with the vinaigrette and season well with the thyme, salt, and pepper, tossing to coat.

Working in batches, grill the vegetables that take the longest to cook and move through the faster-cooking pieces, cooking each until fork-tender. The onion and eggplant will take about 6 minutes per side; the peppers about 4 minutes per side; and the squashes and asparagus will cook the fastest, about 3 minutes per side. Return the vegetables to the baking sheet as they're finished.

Arrange all the vegetables on a platter and serve warm or at room temperature.

DOUGHS

WHOLE WHEAT PIZZA DOUGH

A healthier, slightly more toothsome alternative to the classic, this dough could be used in place of any recipe calling for the NY Style Pizza Dough (page 98).

2¼ cups (280 g) all-purpose flour, plus more for dusting

1¼ cups (155 g) whole wheat flour

1¼ cups (300 ml) warm water (110°F/43°C), plus more as needed

1¼ teaspoons instant yeast

2 teaspoons kosher salt

Extra-virgin olive oil, for greasing

MAKES THREE 9-OZ (250-G) BALLS OF DOUGH; ENOUGH FOR THREE 12-INCH (30-CM) PIZZAS

In a large bowl, stir together both flours and the water just until combined. Cover and set aside for 30 minutes. Using your hands, mix in the yeast and then the salt. Transfer the dough to a lightly floured surface and knead until the dough is soft and springy, about 7 minutes. (Alternatively, mix and knead the dough in the bowl of a stand mixer using the dough hook.)

Divide the dough into 3 equal pieces, each about 9 oz (250 g). Form each piece into a tight ball.

Lightly oil a baking dish that is large enough for the dough balls to rise. Arrange the dough balls in the dish, rub each dough ball lightly with olive oil, then cover loosely with plastic wrap. Set aside at room temperature to rise until doubled in size and the surface becomes bubbly, about 4 hours. The dough is now ready to use in the pizza recipe of your choice.

Alternatively, let rise for 1 hour, then refrigerate overnight; remove from the refrigerator 3 hours before baking. (After rising for 1 hour, the dough can also be individually wrapped with plastic wrap and frozen for up to 1 month; let thaw completely and come to room temperature before using.)

NY STYLE PIZZA DOUGH

Producing a thin, crisp crust that's slightly chewy, this dough is an all-purpose winner. It can be used for nearly any combination of toppings or for a grilled pizza or calzone. To turn this classic dough into a crust flecked with herbs, stir 2 tablespoons chopped fresh oregano, thyme, basil, or rosemary (or 1 tablespoon crumbled dried herbs) into the dough.

3½ cups (430 g) all-purpose flour, plus more for dusting

1¼ cups (300 ml) warm water (110°F/43°C), plus more as needed

1¼ teaspoons instant yeast

2 teaspoons kosher salt

Extra-virgin olive oil, for greasing

MAKES THREE 9-OZ (250-G) BALLS OF DOUGH; ENOUGH FOR THREE 12-INCH (30-CM) PIZZAS

In a large bowl, stir together the flour and water until just combined. Cover and set aside for 30 minutes. Using your hands, mix in the yeast and then the salt. Transfer the dough to a lightly floured surface and knead until the dough is soft and springy, about 7 minutes. (Alternatively, mix and knead the dough in the bowl of a stand mixer using the dough hook.)

Divide the dough into 3 equal pieces, each about 9 oz (250 g). Form each piece into a tight ball.

Lightly oil a baking dish that is large enough for the dough balls to rise. Arrange the dough balls in the dish, rub each dough ball lightly with olive oil, then cover loosely with plastic wrap. Set aside at room temperature to rise until doubled in size and the surface becomes bubbly, about 3 hours. The dough is now ready to use in the pizza recipe of your choice.

Alternatively, let rise for 1 hour, then refrigerate overnight; remove from the refrigerator 3 hours before baking. (After rising for 1 hour, the dough can also be individually wrapped with plastic wrap and frozen for up to 1 month; let thaw completely and come to room temperature before using.)

GLUTEN-FREE PIZZA DOUGH

**This versatile dough couldn't be simpler to make. It can be prebaked
in advance, providing an easy alternative for gluten-free guests.
It works well with any of the pizza recipes in the book.**

1 cup (240 ml) warm water
(110°F/43°C)

1 tablespoon extra-virgin olive oil,
plus more for greasing

1 envelope (2¼ teaspoons)
instant yeast

1 teaspoon sugar

3 cups (350 g)

all-purpose gluten-free flour
blend, plus more for dusting

2½ teaspoons kosher salt

**MAKES TWO 10-OZ (285-G)
BALLS OF DOUGH; ENOUGH
FOR TWO 11-INCH (28-CM)
PIZZAS**

In the bowl of a stand mixer, whisk together the water, olive oil, yeast, and sugar. Set aside until foamy, about 10 minutes.

Add the flour to the yeast mixture. Using the paddle attachment, beat on low speed until combined, about 2 minutes. Add the salt and mix on medium speed until well combined, about 2 minutes. Reduce the speed to low and mix for 2 minutes. The dough will be thick and sticky. Transfer to an oiled bowl, cover, and refrigerate for at least 1 hour or up to 3 hours.

Remove the dough from the refrigerator 30 minutes before baking. Divide the dough into 2 equal pieces, each about 10 oz (285 g). Form each piece into a ball. The dough is now ready to use in the pizza recipe of your choice. (The dough can also be individually wrapped with plastic wrap and frozen for up to 1 month; let thaw completely and come to room temperature for about 2 hours before using.)

When ready to bake, preheat the oven to 450°F/230°C. Lightly oil a large rimless baking sheet.

On a flour-dusted work surface, roll out 1 ball of dough into an 11-inch (28-cm) circle. Transfer to the prepared baking sheet and let rest for 15 minutes. Partially bake the crust just until set, turning once halfway through, about 9 minutes. Remove from the oven and top the pizza with toppings, if using, then return to the oven and bake until golden brown, about 10 minutes longer. Repeat with the remaining dough ball.

CAULIFLOWER PIZZA CRUST

Both gluten-free and grain-free, this cauliflower crust can be used with
any of the sauce and topping combinations in the book. The addition of
cheese helps bind the crust and gives it great flavor.

1 head cauliflower, thick stems
removed, cut into small florets

3 tablespoons almond flour

3 tablespoons grated
Parmesan cheese

3 tablespoons shredded
mozzarella cheese

1 tablespoon extra-virgin olive oil,
plus more for brushing

1 teaspoon kosher salt

½ teaspoon dried basil

½ teaspoon garlic powder

1 large egg yolk

**MAKES ONE 9-INCH (23-CM)
PIZZA CRUST**

Position an oven rack in the middle of the oven and place a pizza stone on the rack. Preheat the oven to 450°F/230°C. Once the oven has reached 450°F/230°C, let the stone continue to heat for 15–30 minutes longer, without opening the door.

Put the cauliflower in a food processor and pulse until the florets are evenly chopped into tiny snowflake-like pieces, about 30 pulses. Transfer to a microwave-safe bowl, cover the bowl with a damp paper towel, and microwave on high for 5 minutes. Pour the cauliflower onto a kitchen towel. Using a wooden spoon, spread it out so that all the steam can escape. Once cooled, wrap it tightly in the towel and squeeze out as much moisture as you can. This is important because otherwise, the crust won't hold together when baked.

Transfer the cauliflower to a large bowl and add the almond flour, Parmesan, mozzarella, olive oil, salt, basil, garlic powder, and egg yolk. Stir well to combine. Cut a 12-inch (30-cm) piece of parchment paper, place it on a pizza peel, and brush it lightly with olive oil. Turn the dough out onto the oiled paper. Using your hands, form the dough into a 9-inch (23-cm) circle, pressing gently and making sure to keep the edges from cracking.

Carefully slide the crust and parchment from the peel onto the hot stone in the oven and bake for 10 minutes. Using the peel, remove the crust from the oven.

The crust can now be topped with the sauce and toppings of your choice, then returned to the pizza stone to bake for about 5 minutes. Using the peel, transfer the pizza to a cutting board, let cool for a few minutes, then slice and serve right away.

SHEET PAN PIZZA DOUGH

Thick, fluffy, focaccia–like sheet pan dough is the easiest dough to make, and the kids will love to lend a hand. The dough can be prebaked well before dinnertime and can also be partially baked and frozen for up to a month—perfect for last–minute meals.

1⅓ cups (325 ml) warm water (110°F/43°C)

1 tablespoon instant yeast

1 tablespoon sugar

3½ cups (405 g) all-purpose flour, plus more for dusting

2 teaspoons kosher salt

2 tablespoons extra–virgin olive oil, plus more for greasing

MAKES 2 LB (1 KG) DOUGH; ENOUGH FOR 1 LARGE SHEET PAN PIZZA

In a medium bowl, whisk together the water, yeast, and sugar. Set aside until foamy, about 10 minutes. In a large bowl, stir together the flour and salt. Add the yeast mixture and olive oil to the flour mixture. Using a wooden spoon or your hands, stir the dough until well mixed. The dough should be soft and a bit sticky. Turn out onto a floured surface and, using floured hands, knead until soft, about 3 minutes.

Clean out the large bowl and rub with olive oil. Form the dough into a ball, transfer to the oiled bowl, and cover loosely with plastic wrap. Set aside in a warm, draft-free spot until doubled in size, about 1 hour. The dough is now ready to use in the pizza recipe of your choice.

When ready to bake, oil a 17-by-13-inch (43-by-33-cm) rimmed baking sheet. Transfer the dough to the prepared baking sheet. Gently pull it out to fit the pan; you may need to let it rest for 5–10 minutes if it becomes resistant. Let the dough rise until slightly puffy, about 20 minutes.

Meanwhile, position a rack in the upper third of the oven and preheat to 450°F/230°C. Partially bake the pizza crust for 8 minutes. The crust can now be topped with the sauce and toppings of your choice, then baked until the crust is golden brown, about 18 minutes. Alternatively, wrap the cooled, partially baked pizza crust tightly in plastic wrap and freeze for up to 1 month before topping and baking.

DEEP DISH CORNMEAL PIZZA DOUGH

Baked in a cast-iron pan, this dough emerges crisp on the outside and tender and bready on the inside. It makes a great "container" for thick layers of toppings.

3¾ cups (435 g) bread flour, plus more for dusting

⅔ cup (90 g) medium-grind cornmeal

2 tablespoons sugar

1 tablespoon kosher salt

1 envelope (2¼ teaspoons) instant yeast

1½ cups (350 ml) warm water (110°F/43°C), plus more as needed

5 tablespoons (75 ml) extra-virgin olive oil, plus more for greasing

MAKES TWO 1-LB 3-OZ (540-G) BALLS OF DOUGH; ENOUGH FOR TWO 10-INCH (25-CM) DEEP DISH PIZZAS

In a large bowl, combine the flour, cornmeal, sugar, salt, and yeast. Add the water and olive oil in a steady stream while mixing the dough with a wooden spoon or your hands until the dough comes together in a rough mass. If the dough does not form into a ball, sprinkle with 1–2 teaspoons more water and knead until a rough mass forms. Let rest for 10 minutes.

Transfer the dough to a lightly floured surface and knead for about 1 minute. The dough should be tacky to the touch but not sticky. Divide the dough into 2 equal pieces, each about 1 lb 3 oz (540 g). Form each piece into a smooth ball.

Lightly oil baking dish that is large enough for the dough balls to rise. Arrange the dough balls in the dish, rub each dough ball lightly with olive oil, then cover loosely with plastic wrap. Set aside at room temperature to rise until doubled in size, about 2 hours. The dough is now ready to use in the pizza recipe of your choice.

Alternatively, let rise for 1 hour, then refrigerate overnight; remove from the refrigerator 3 hours before baking. (After rising for 1 hour, the dough can also be individually wrapped with plastic wrap and frozen for up to 1 month; let thaw completely and come to room temperature for about 4 hours before using.)

SAUCES

ALL-PURPOSE PIZZA SAUCE

A quick-to-prepare uncooked tomato sauce adds zing and just the right amount of acidity to your favorite pizza toppings. A splash of balsamic vinegar brightens the flavors while contributing just a touch of sweetness. Make a double batch and freeze whatever you don't use so you'll have a head start on your next pizza night.

1 can (800 g) crushed tomatoes

2 tablespoons balsamic vinegar

2 tablespoons extra-virgin olive oil

2 teaspoons Italian seasoning or dried oregano

MAKES ABOUT 3 CUPS (700 ML)

In a bowl, stir together the tomatoes, vinegar, olive oil, and Italian seasoning.

Use right away or transfer to an airtight container and refrigerate for up to 1 week or freeze for up to 1 month.

CLASSIC BASIL PESTO

This easy sauce makes good use of summer's abundance of fresh basil. It's a snap to put together in the food processor and freezes beautifully. Since a little goes a long way, freeze the pesto in smaller portions to streamline prep on busy weeknights (ice cube trays provide the perfect compartments).

1 clove garlic, chopped

¼ cup (30 g) pine nuts

2 cups (60 g) packed fresh basil leaves

½ cup (120 ml) extra-virgin olive oil

½ cup (60 g) grated Parmesan cheese

Kosher salt and freshly ground pepper

MAKES ABOUT 1 CUP (240 ML)

With a food processor running, drop the garlic through the feed tube and process until minced. Turn off the processor, add the pine nuts, and pulse a few times to chop. Turn off the processor, add the basil, and pulse a few times to chop coarsely. Then, with the processor running, add the olive oil through the feed tube in a slow, steady stream and process until a smooth, moderately thick paste forms, stopping to scrape down the sides of the bowl as needed.

Transfer to a medium bowl and stir in the Parmesan. Season to taste with salt and pepper.

Use right away or transfer to an airtight container, top with a thin layer of oil (to prevent oxidation), and refrigerate for up to 1 week or freeze for up to 1 month.

ROASTED RED PEPPER PESTO

Sweet roasted red bell peppers and toasted walnuts star in this well-balanced sauce. Try swapping the walnuts for toasted almonds if you like, and to save time, use jarred roasted bell peppers.

2 red bell peppers

1 clove garlic, minced

1/2 cup (60 g) walnuts halves, toasted and roughly chopped

1/4 cup (30 g) grated Parmesan cheese

3 tablespoons extra-virgin olive oil

Kosher salt and freshly ground pepper

**MAKES ABOUT
1 1/2 CUPS (350 ML)**

Using tongs or a large fork, hold 1 bell pepper at a time directly over the flame of a gas burner, or place directly on the grate. Roast, turning as needed, until blistered and charred black on all sides, 10–15 minutes total. (Alternatively, place the peppers under a preheated broiler, as close as possible to the heating element, and roast to char them on all sides, turning as needed.)

Transfer the peppers to a bowl, cover with plastic wrap or a kitchen towel, and set aside to steam until cooled, about 20 minutes. Once cool, peel or rub away the charred skins, then seed the peppers and cut into chunks.

In a food processor or blender, combine the roasted peppers, garlic, walnuts, cheese, and olive oil and processs until smooth. Stop the machine and taste the pesto; adjust the seasoning with salt and pepper, pulsing to mix.

Use right away or transfer to an airtight container and refrigerate for up to 1 week or freeze for up to 1 month.

SPICY ARRABIATA SAUCE

Arrabiata sauce is typically used as a simple Roman–style pasta sauce but tastes delicious atop any pizza when you want a little extra spice.

1 tablespoon extra–virgin olive oil

½ small yellow onion, finely chopped

1 clove garlic, minced

1 can (800 g) crushed tomatoes

2 teaspoons minced Calabrian chiles in oil

1 teaspoon sugar

Kosher salt and freshly ground pepper

**MAKES ABOUT
3 CUPS (700 ML)**

In a large frying pan over medium heat, warm the olive oil. Add the onion and cook, stirring occasionally, until tender, about 4 minutes. Add the garlic and cook, stirring occasionally, just until fragrant, about 30 seconds. Add the tomatoes, Calabrian chiles, and sugar and cook, stirring occasionally, until the sauce is slightly reduced, about 7 minutes. Season to taste with salt and pepper.

Use right away or let cool to room temperature, then transfer to an airtight container and refrigerate for up to 1 week or freeze for up to 1 month.

OLIVE TAPENADE

Olive tapenade works wonders on hot, crisp pizza dough. Choose what you pair with it selectively—because olives are so salty, it's best to use milder cheese and other ingredients that aren't naturally salty themselves.
Leftover tapenade is terrific served with crostini and goat cheese.

1 clove garlic, minced

2 oil-packed anchovies, rinsed

1½ cups (210 g) pitted brine-cured olives (black, green, or a mixture)

¼ cup (7 g) loosely packed fresh herb leaves, such as thyme, oregano, or basil, or a mixture

Grated zest of 1 lemon

3 tablespoons extra-virgin olive oil

⅛ teaspoon red pepper flakes (optional)

**MAKES ABOUT
1¼ CUPS (300 ML)**

In a food processor, combine the garlic and anchovies and pulse to mince. Add the olives, herbs, lemon zest, olive oil, and red pepper flakes, if using. Process until the texture is to your liking, either to a coarse or smooth purée.

Use right away or transfer to an airtight container and refrigerate for up to 2 weeks.

CREAMY GARLIC SAUCE

The base of this terrific all-purpose white sauce is ricotta cheese, which provides structure and flavor. It makes a great change from the classic tomato sauce. Select a whole-milk, smooth-textured ricotta for the best results.

2 tablespoons extra-virgin olive oil

½ yellow onion, minced

3 cloves garlic, minced

Kosher salt and freshly ground pepper

1 cup (225 g) whole-milk ricotta cheese

¼ cup (60 ml) heavy cream

1 teaspoon minced fresh oregano

**MAKES ABOUT
1¼ CUPS (300 ML)**

In a small frying pan over medium-low heat, warm the olive oil. Add the onion and garlic and season with salt and pepper. Cook, stirring occasionally, until the onion is tender, about 4 minutes, taking care not to let the onion or garlic brown. Transfer the contents of the pan, including all of the oil, to a small bowl and let cool.

When the onion mixture is cool, stir in the ricotta, cream, and oregano. Taste and season with more salt and pepper, if needed.

Use right away or transfer to an airtight container and refrigerate for up to 3 days or freeze for up to 1 month.

BARBECUE SAUCE

Homemade barbecue sauce is infinitely better than most store-bought versions and gives you the flexibility to personalize it to your tastes. Whether you like yours more or less sweet, or abundantly spicy (or not), feel free to adjust the seasonings as you desire.

2 cups (450 g) tomato ketchup

3 tablespoons dark brown sugar

3 tablespoons apple cider vinegar

2 tablespoons yellow mustard

2 tablespoons Worcestershire sauce

2 teaspoons smoked paprika

1½ teaspoons kosher salt

1 teaspoon garlic powder

½ teaspoon onion powder

½ teaspoon freshly ground pepper

**MAKES ABOUT
3 CUPS (700 ML)**

In a small saucepan over high heat, combine the ketchup, brown sugar, vinegar, mustard, Worcestershire sauce, paprika, salt, garlic powder, onion powder, and pepper and bring to a boil. Reduce the heat to medium-low and simmer, stirring occasionally, until slightly thickened, about 20 minutes.

Use right away or transfer to an airtight container and refrigerate for up to 2 weeks.

INDEX

PIZZA

DELICIOUS RECIPES FOR ANYTIME

Conceived and produced by Weldon Owen International
in collaboration with Williams Sonoma, Inc.
3250 Van Ness Avenue, San Francisco, CA 94109

weldon**owen**

an imprint of Insight Editions
P.O. Box 3088
San Rafael, CA 94912
www.weldonowen.com

ISBN: 979-8-88674-154-4

Manufactured in China by Insight Editions
10 9 8 7 6 5 4 3 2 1

CEO Raoul Goff
VP Publisher Roger Shaw
Associate Publisher Amy Marr
Publishing Director Katie Killebrew
VP Creative Chrissy Kwasnik
Design Manager Megan Sinead Bingham
Production Designer Jean Hwang
Sr Production Manager Joshua Smith
Sr Production Manager, Subsidiary Rights
 Lina s Palma-Temena

Photographer and Prop Stylist Erin Scott
Images on pages 7, 8–9, 23, 43, 50, 60, 66,
 73, 86, 92, 94, 97, 100, 113, 116–117, 122, 125
 photographed by Erin Kunkel
Food Stylist Lillian Kang

Weldon Owen would also like to thank
Kris Balloun, Jessica Easto, Kim Laidlaw,
and Elizabeth Parson.

Insight Editions, in association with Roots of Peace, will plant two trees for each tree used in the manufacturing of this book. Roots of Peace is an internationally renowned humanitarian organization dedicated to eradicating land mines worldwide and converting war-torn lands into productive farms and wildlife habitats. Roots of Peace will plant two million fruit and nut trees in Afghanistan and provide farmers there with the skills and support necessary for sustainable land use.